ONLINE LAW

for journalists, web editors, PRs and
anyone who publishes on the internet

Cleland Thom

CLELANDTHOM●●●

clelandthom.co.uk
onlinelawforjournalists.co.uk

Clean Copy
Editor | Book Designer | Publisher
cleancopy.co.uk

ONLINE LAW FOR JOURNALISTS

Cover design and formatting: Clean Copy Publishing

Published by Clean Copy
Editor | Book Designer | Publisher
cleancopy.co.uk
cleancopypublishing@gmail.com

All content enquiries to cleland@collegeofmediaandpublishing.co.uk

First published 2016

ISBN-13: 978-1530848454

ISBN-10: 1530848458

You can access additional material on the

Online Law website

www.onlinelawforjournalists.co.uk

The site contains a useful blog on online law developments.

Online Law book owners can also use the exclusive Student Resource Area. Please email cleland@collegeofmediaanadpublishing.co.uk for your password to access it.

Additional copies of the book Online Law for Journalists can be purchased at these outlets:

Amazon Paperback and Kindle

CreateSpace estore Paperback:
https://www.createspace.com/6180446

Students may be eligible for a discount. Contact cleland@collegeofmediaanadpublishing.co.uk

About Cleland Thom

Cleland Thom is a consultant and trainer in media and internet law.

Between 1992 and 2002, he lectured in media law at three colleges delivering courses accredited by the National Council for the Training of Journalists, the Broadcast Journalism Training Council and the Periodicals Training Council.

He started a training and consultancy business in 2003 and, since then, his clients have included the Manchester Evening News, RBI Magazines, Big Issue North, Smooth Radio, and Waitrose.

He is the Press Gazette's legal blogger (pressgazette.co.uk) and has trained more than 2,500 people in media and internet law. They include directors, editors, heads of comms, producers, journalists and PR / comms staff working for public authorities, corporations, newspapers, magazines, websites, TV and radio stations.

He has dealt with more than 7,000 pre-publication legal queries, and framed more than 100 challenges to court reporting restrictions.

He is author of several previous publications, including Election Law for Journalists and Internet Law for Journalists.

Cleland is also principal of the College of Media and Publishing, and lives in West Sussex.

Contact Cleland Thom

For information about Cleland's media law training and consultancy services, visit:

http://www.clelandthom.co.uk/legal-services/

Cleland is also available on:

LinkedIn: clelandthom

Email: cleland@collegeofmediaandpublishing.co.uk

Dedication

To my sons, Olly, Barney and Jake, who give me so much friendship, help and support, both in my professional and personal life.

Acknowledgements

My grateful thanks go to Jennie Harborth, of Clean Copy Publishing, who edited and published this book, and to Rachel Finnegan, of Irish Academic Editing, who proofread it.

Review

The book covers all the major issues about which journalists should be aware. It is a clear and concise guide in clear and concise language, with handy case studies and examples highlighting points.

Mike Dodd, *Editor, Media Lawyer*

Review

Cleland Thom is our first choice for providing essential and authoritative legal checking for our investigative stories.

His book will prove invaluable in updating readers' legal knowledge in a fast-changing journalistic world.

It is comprehensive but structured so it is easy to understand. Highly recommended.

Kevin Gopal, *Editor, Big Issue North*

Review

A concise and illuminating guide to what is becoming increasingly difficult terrain for the media and others to traverse.

The rise of digital media poses special legal and ethical problems for journalists, bloggers and ordinary citizens, but Cleland Thom cuts through the haze to offer insight into how to operate safely in the new landscape.

His case studies ranging from the copyright of Tweets to the dangers of posts left on message boards are both fascinating and bang up to date.

Cleland brilliantly uses such examples to highlight the challenges many of us face in trying to steer our way through complex online legal issues.

Dave Porter, *Programme leader, BA Multimedia Journalism, Manchester Metropolitan University*

Review

Cleland's knowledge in this area is second to none and has already been immensely important in my world of broadcasting.

For journalists, too, having this by your side will give a reassuring sense of security.

Graham Dene, *Presenter, BBC Sussex and Surrey. Former presenter of Capital Radio's breakfast show*

Review

This book offers a succinct starting point for anyone publishing online who wants to know if they are about to run into a legal firewall.

Kirsten Sjøvoll, *Member of Matrix Chambers, specialising in media and information law*

ABBREVIATIONS

Abbreviations used throughout this book are:

UK   United Kingdom

EU   European Union

US   United States of America

Ipso   Independent Press Standards Organisation

Ofcom   Office of Communications

All other abbreviations are addressed per chapter and are listed in the Appendix at the end.

CONTENTS

ONLINE LAW

For journalists, bloggers, PRs and anyone who publishes on the internet

INTRODUCTION

The internet caught this country's legal system unawares. Legal precedents and statutes, some dating back centuries, suddenly had to relate to modern technology. Many of them were inadequate, and the courts and the government have spent the last 15 years or so catching up.

A publisher used to be someone who published books, newspapers or magazines. However, now, anyone who runs a blog, comments on a forum, or posts on Twitter is a publisher, and is subject to the same laws as journalists. The publishing public is now getting used to the fact that internet publishing is not some virtual wild west, where anything goes.

WHAT HAPPENED TO FREE SPEECH?

Journalism has more laws and regulations restricting what can be said and done than almost any other profession and, therefore, the concept of a "free press" is a myth. In this country, people are only able to write freely after first obeying a significant number of laws and regulatory requirements.

For instance, the media's right to publish people's personal information and photographs has been curtailed since the

European Convention on Human Rights (ECHR) was introduced into UK law by the Human Rights Act 1998.

Journalists aged over 50 will recall a "golden" era when the media was relatively free to "publish and be damned". Now, many would reword this phrase as "be damned – and then publish."

Journalists must now consider, before they publish, whether their words, photographs and other content could breach people's privacy rights and, if they do, whether demonstrable public interest exists.

Their cause is not helped by the fact that the definition of public interest, used by the media regulator's Independent Press Standards Organisation and the Office of Communications, and by the Data Protection Act, is stricter than that used in English common law prior to the introduction of the ECHR.

Lord Denning, as master of the rolls, said in 1969, in the Court of Appeal judgment in the case London Artists Ltd v Littler, that public interest should not to be confined within narrow limits. He said: "Whenever a matter is such as to affect people at large so that they may be legitimately interested in, or concerned at, what is going on or what may happen to them or others, then it is a matter of public interest, on which everyone is entitled to make honest comment" (UK Parliament House of Lords, n.d., *Judgments – Reynolds v. Times Newspapers Limited and Others*).

This discrepancy was dealt with, to a limited extent, by a revision of the Editors' Code of Practice (the code), introduced on 1 January, 2016. The code can be viewed here: https://www.ipso.co.uk/IPSO/cop.html

The revision extended the scope of the public interest defence, which now may be available in the following circumstances:

1. Detecting or exposing crime or the threat of crime, or serious impropriety.

2. Protecting public health or safety.

3. Protecting the public from being misled by an action or statement of an individual or organisation.

4. Disclosing a person or organisation's failure or likely failure to comply with any obligation to which they are subject.

5. Disclosing a miscarriage of justice.

6. Raising or contributing to a matter of public debate, including serious cases of impropriety, unethical conduct, or incompetence concerning the public.

7. Disclosing concealment, or likely concealment, of any of the above.

The public interest defence became harder for journalists to use in 2009. The code was revised to say: "Editors invoking the public interest will need to demonstrate that they reasonably believed publication – or journalistic activity taken with a view to publication – would both serve, and be proportionate to, the public interest and explain how they reached that decision at the time" (Ipso, 2015, *Editors' Code of Practice*).

This means that journalists must be certain what the public interest issue is when they begin investigating a story, and must be able to back their decision with evidence.

This can pose problems to investigative journalists who sometimes need to carry out preliminary enquiries to determine whether a story stands up. They may not be certain if there is a public interest issue at this stage.

THERE IS NO RIGHT TO FREE SPEECH

In addition, the UK does not provide any legal or constitutional guarantee to safeguard the free press. This contrasts with the US, where the First Amendment of the US constitution sets out that: "Congress shall make no law […] abridging the freedom of speech, or of the press […]" (National Constitution Center, n.d., *Amendment I Freedom of religion, speech, press, assembly, and petition*).

David Cameron's Conservative government mooted a constitutional right to a free press in its proposed bill of rights.

However, this is now by no means certain, following the UK's decision to leave the European Union. The impact of Brexit on all aspects of UK law remains to be seen, and is discussed in the next chapter.

In the meantime, journalists and online publishers must contend with dozens of pieces of legislation and two regulatory codes, making journalism one of the most legally restricted professions there is.

So, this book looks at media law and regulation against a background where our media is more heavily restricted than it has ever been. This is borne out by the fact that the UK is listed 38th, behind countries such as Chile, Ghana and Uruguay, in the 2016 World Press Freedom Index – down 18 places from 2015 (Reporters Without Borders, 2016, *2016 World Press Freedom Index*).

However, those who blame the constraints of European law and the ECHR for the UK's ranking should bear in mind that our European neighbour Holland is second.

In November 2016, independent freedom watchdog Freedom House published a report entitled, "Silencing the Messenger: Communication Apps Under Pressure", which said that that internet freedom around the world declined in 2016 for the sixth consecutive year (Freedom House, 2016, *Silencing the Messenger: Communication Apps Under Pressure*).

It said that that increasing numbers of governments were targeting social media and communication apps as a means of halting the rapid dissemination of information, particularly during anti-government protests.

THE IMPACT OF BREXIT

EU law will continue to be applicable in the UK until the UK leaves the EU. However, the legal situation after that depends on the outcome of the UK's Brexit negotiations.

Prime Minister Theresa May is introducing the great repeal bill, which seeks to end the authority of EU law by converting all its provisions into British law on the day the UK leaves the EU. The 1972 European Communities Act will simultaneously be repealed.

After that, it is almost certain that the UK will allow existing EU laws to remain in place, unless there is a need to change them. If there is, then parliament will introduce new legislation.

The reality is that Brexit it unlikely to have any significant effect on UK media law and regulation in the medium term. The main affected areas are copyright, trademarks, the ECHR, data protection, and defamation.

Let us look at these in turn.

COPYRIGHT

The EU has certainly helped to shape UK copyright law, especially over the past 15 years, both through legislation and EU court decisions.

For instance, in 2015, the European Court of Justice (ECJ) ruled in the case Pez Hejduk v EnergieAgentur that photographers can sue for copyright breaches in the UK courts if their photographs are used in another EU country. In the past, actions had to be brought in the country where they were published.

It is unclear whether historic ECJ rulings like this will carry any weight post-Brexit. The UK certainly will not be bound by future ones.

Much UK copyright law has been derived from EU directives that have been implemented through UK legislation. Although the great repeal bill will end the jurisdiction of the ECJ in the UK, these directives will remain the same unless parliament repeals them, or introduces new legislation. However, this is unlikely, given the global nature of copyright in the digital age.

The UK will not have to implement future directives, and that could be significant in the long term. There are EU copyright reforms on the horizon designed to achieve greater harmony between member states. Some differences are inevitable if the UK decides not to replicate them.

However, it is important to remember that many UK copyright principles are based on international treaties that go beyond the EU. The UK will remain a member of the World Intellectual Property Organisation, a global forum for intellectual property (IP) services and cooperation among UN members. As a result, fundamental change is unlikely.

TRADEMARKS

EU trademarks will no longer be applicable in the UK, post-Brexit, and will apply only to countries within the EU. It is expected that UK law will be amended to provide equivalent trademark rights in the UK with the same specifications, priority dates and terms as specified in the current EU arrangements.

DATA PROTECTION

Journalists rarely encounter the Data Protection Act (DPA), as "journalistic exemption" gives them immunity from most of its requirements.

The DPA is a UK law, and so will be unaffected by Brexit. However, ECJ judgments about the act will be binding, at least until the UK leaves the EU.

The UK will have to abide by the EU's updated General Data Protection Regulation (GDPR) from May 2018. This law applies to organisations in any country that collect and use EU citizens' personal information. Thus, any UK media with an EU readership may be affected.

One key change was revealed in guidelines published by the EU's Article 29 working party in December 2016.

Public authorities, and businesses above a certain size, will have to appoint a mandatory data protection officer and some will have to budget for recruiting a new member of staff, or outsource the role (European Commission, 2016, *Guidelines on Data Protection Officers*).The EU's "cookie law", which has led to media displaying cookie consent boxes on their websites, will remain in force for the time being.

However, it is unlikely that the UK will implement the updated version, which is due be introduced before 2020. This means that webmasters may be able to remove these consent boxes, unless the UK parliament introduces its own cookie legislation.

The future relationship between the media and the DPA remains uncertain, with or without Brexit. The Information Commissioner reassured the media in 2014 that he had no intention of interfering with the freedom of the media. He said that the data protection regime was not intended to obstruct a free and fair press.

However, the Information Commissioner's Office's (ICO) media guidelines about the DPA stress that the journalistic exemption only applies to journalistic activity carried out in the public interest. The guidelines say: "You must reasonably believe publication is in the public interest – and that the public interest justifies the extent of the intrusion into private life" (ICO, 2016, *Data protection and journalism media guidance.pdf*).

In recent years, celebrities like Cheryl Fernandez-Versini's ex-husband Jean Bernard (The Telegraph, 2017, *Cheryl Fernandez-Versini's husband wins magazine privacy damages*) and musician Paul Weller (The Guardian, 2014, *Paul Weller children win privacy damages over photos on Mail Online*)are among celebrities who have won damages under the act. The DPA features on most writs issued against the media these days, now that the Defamation Act 2013 has made libel actions harder to win.

Editors are likely to see more challenges to the journalistic exemption on public interest grounds in future. And the media may be better placed to defend its traditional freedoms without interference from the ECJ. This means that Brexit may turn out to be an advantage in this respect.

DEFAMATION

Reader comments on message boards are currently protected by the EU Electronic Commerce Directive (ECD) Regulations 2002.

This law means publishers are not liable if a reader defames someone or breaks another law, provided the publisher:

1. Does not moderate or edit the content, and

2. Operates a "report and remove" system where offensive posts are removed quickly on receipt of a complaint.

If the UK decides not to continue with the ECD, then defamatory comments will not be affected, as our own Defamation Acts of 1996 and 2013 provide similar defences.

However, the UK would need to introduce its own act extending "report and remove" to breaches of other laws.

This might be a good thing, as there are signs that the EU may water down the ECD's protection. This situation must be seen alongside a surprise decision by the European Court of Human Rights in the case Delfi AS v Estonia (BAILII, ECHR 586, 2015).

This case, coupled with the possibility of the EU introducing a "duty of care" for website operators, may mean the UK could decide to introduce a law that preserves the existing arrangements on non-moderation and "report and remove".

EUROPEAN CONVENTION ON HUMAN RIGHTS (ECHR)

European citizens possess the right to the freedom of expression under the ECHR but, again, this freedom has limitations. On the one hand, article 10 says: "Everyone has the right to freedom of expression. This right shall include freedom to hold opinions and to receive and impart information and ideas without interference by public authority […]" (UK Legislation, n.d., *Human Rights Act*).

However, the ECHR also says: "The exercise of these freedoms, […] may be subject to such formalities, conditions, restrictions or penalties as are prescribed by law and are necessary in a democratic society, in the interests of national security, territorial integrity or public safety, […] for the protection of the reputation or rights of others, for preventing the disclosure of information received in confidence […]"(UK Legislation, n.d., *Human Rights Act*).

It is too early to predict how Brexit will affect the UK's relationship with the ECHR, and how any changes will affect the media.

THE MEDIA'S REGULATORY BODIES

In the UK, the Independent Press Standards Organisation regulates newspapers and magazines and their websites, while the Office of Communications regulates commercial radio and TV. The British Broadcasting Corporation's (BBC) editorial content, including its magazines, is subject to the BBC's editorial guidelines.

INDEPENDENT PRESS STANDARDS ORGANISATION (IPSO)

Ipso replaced the Press Complaints Commission (PCC) on 8 September 2014 following recommendations made by the Leveson inquiry.

Ipso administers the Editors' Code of Practice and investigates and rules on alleged breaches. It has the power to:

1. Monitor printed media and their websites.
2. Mediate and adjudicate complaints about breaches of the code.
3. Require publication of corrections and adjudications.
4. Issue fines for serious and systemic failings.
5. Intervene on behalf of the public over privacy and harassment issues.

Publishers must provide complaints procedures and ensure that management and editorial staff members know how to apply them.

If Ipso receives a complaint, it refers the complainant to the publication to deal with under its own complaints procedures.

The publication's editor must deal with more serious complaints within a 28-day deadline.

If the complainant and the editor cannot reach an agreement, Ipso will investigate and may adjudicate in the event of a possible breach of the code.

The Editors' Code of Practice can be seen here:

https://www.ipso.co.uk/IPSO/cop.html

(Ipso, 2015, *Editors' Code of Practice*).

Landmark adjudications by the PCC may also still be relevant, unless they have been superseded.

Ipso has published a book called The Editors' Codebook, which explains how it has interpreted the editors' code, and sets out best practice guidelines for journalists.

The Editors' Codebook can be downloaded as a PDF here:

http://www.editorscode.org.uk/downloads/codebook/codebook-2016.pdf

The codebook states that although Ipso is not bound by previous PCC decisions, key PCC cases are included where they are still relevant.

In February 2016, Ipso asked retired civil servant Sir Joseph Pilling to review its independence, effectiveness and funding. Sir Joseph published his report, "The External Ipso Review", in October 2016. It made nearly 50 recommendations covering most aspects of the regulator's work.

The External Ipso Review report can be downloaded here: http://www.ipsoreview.co.uk/

Case study

In October 2016, Ipso rejected a privacy complaint from a grieving father after the Sun newspaper published photographs and comments from his Facebook page without his permission, following his son's suicide(Ipso, 2016, *03446-16 McHale v The Sun*); (The Sun, 2016, *Dad's anger after commuters refused to help son*).

Ipso's complaints committee said John McHale had publicly disclosed information, and published publicly viewable posts on social media about the death, including pictures of his family.

It did not consider that republishing the posts and photographs in the article represented an unjustified intrusion into his private life.

OFFICE OF COMMUNICATIONS (OFCOM)

Ofcom provides detailed guidelines intended for the maintenance of TV and radio broadcasting standards, and it will also deal with complaints.

The Ofcom code can be downloaded here:

http://stakeholders.ofcom.org.uk/broadcasting/broadcast-codes/broadcast-code/

DEFAMATION

Defamation is a constant risk for publishers.

For example, in July 2016, the Daily Mail apologised for publishing an article which said: "An article published on May 26 described Lord Sugar as a 'spiv'. This word may be understood to describe a person who is dishonest in his business dealings. We are happy to confirm that this was not the intended meaning, as indeed the article stated he is honest and hard working" (Press Gazette, 2016, *Likening Alan Sugar to "spiv" Sir Philip Green in headline costs Daily Mail £20,000*).

Lord Sugar later tweeted "The scum @DailyMailUK now humiliated had to pay me 20k for calling me a spiv. I will donate this to GOSH. Enjoy!"

This case demonstrates one of the key areas of defamation law: the meanings of words.

WHAT IS DEFAMATION?

Defamation law exists to protect people and businesses from untrue attacks on their moral or professional reputation. If anyone publishes a statement claiming, for example, that someone is guilty of criminal, unprofessional or antisocial behaviour, the publisher can be sued and may have to pay substantial court damages unless they can prove the allegations are substantially true.

Case study

In June 2015, the comedian Freddie Starr lost a libel action to a woman named Karin Ward who said he groped her

> when she was 15. Her allegations were published on BBC, ITV, on a website and in an ebook. He lost the case because the judge ruled that the allegations were true (Courts and Tribunals Judiciary, 2015, *Freddie Starr v Karin Ward*).

Defamation cases usually involve statements such as:

1. She is a liar.
2. He has committed a crime.
3. She took a bribe.
4. He misused his position for personal gain.
5. She is violent or abusive.
6. He is a paedophile.
7. She had an illicit affair.
8. He took illegal drugs.

A person who starts a libel action is called the claimant, and the person defending it is called the defendant. Cases are tried without a jury unless a court orders otherwise.

WHAT IS A DEFAMATORY STATEMENT?

The Defamation Act (DA) 2013 states that a statement is defamatory if, on the balance of probability, it caused or is likely to cause serious harm to the claimant's reputation (UK Legislation, n.d., *Defamation Act 2013*).

A defamatory statement is one that tends to:

1. Cause someone to be shunned and avoided.
2. Lower them in the eyes of right thinking people.
3. Expose them to ridicule, hatred and contempt.
4. Disparage them in their office, trade or profession.

The words 'tend to' are important, as they mean libel claimants do not have to prove that any of these things actually happened. This gives claimants a distinct advantage in a libel case.

The DA raised the threshold for a libel claim from 'harm' to 'serious harm', and there was some uncertainty about what difference this would make. Most pre-DA libel claimants probably took the view that defamatory publications caused them serious harm.

However, early indications are that the change has reduced the number of libel actions. Research by Thomson Reuters showed there was a 27% fall in 2014 (Press Gazette, 2015, *Research finds 27 per cent drop*).

Case study

The courts have begun to provide some clarity on the issue of what constitutes serious harm. The first case to consider it was Cooke & Midland Heart Limited v MGN Limited & Trinity Mirror Midlands Limited.

The judge, Lord Justice Bean, cited instances of people being called terrorists or paedophiles as examples of 'serious harm'.

He added: "I do not accept that, in every case, evidence will be required to satisfy the serious harm test. Some statements are so obviously likely to cause serious harm to a person's reputation that this likelihood can be inferred" (BAILII, EWHC 2831, 2014).

Case study

In another case, Lachaux v Independent Print Limited (BAILII, EWHC 2242, 2015), Mr Justice Warby suggested that 'serious harm' was something that should be decided as a preliminary issue, before the trial starts.

These preliminary hearings could consider evidence from witnesses to establish whether 'serious harm' has occurred.

However, this case was due to be reviewed by the Court of Appeal this year (2016).

Case study

In the case Theedom v Nourish Training (BAILII, EWHC 3769, 2015), Judge Moloney gave the following guidelines. He said that serious harm:

1. Must be proved, on top of all previous common law requirements for a libel action.

2. Relates to reputation, not injury to feelings.

3. Can be established with or without evidence.

Claimants can try to establish it without evidence from the level of the defamatory meaning of the words, and the nature and extent of the publication.

Further cases are needed before we can draw clearer conclusions as to what constitutes serious reputational harm. However, it seems certain that claimants will stand a better chance of establishing 'seriousness', if they can provide evidence, unless seriousness is obvious from the words and their context.

WHO CAN START A DEFAMATION ACTION?

Any living individual can sue any other living individual for defamation. Libelling dead people, a rarely-used criminal offence, was abolished by the Ministry of Justice in July 2009.

Case study

In 2014, the European Court of Human Rights (ECtHR) ruled that a libellous attack on a dead person could damage the surviving family's reputation to the point where it interfered with their private life, in breach of article 8 of the ECHR. The case that was brought against Ukraine by Mr Vladlen Putistin over an article that indirectly criticised his dead father's role in the infamous 'world war two death march', which inspired the famous film Escape to Victory (ECtHR, 2013, *Case of Putistin v. Ukraine*).

A business can sue if a statement caused or is likely to cause it serious financial loss. However, it must be able to prove its losses so, therefore, a publisher facing a libel threat from a business may be able to request details about the losses.

Again, this area of the DA will remain unclear until there are more rulings by the courts. There has only been one significant one so far, Brett Wilson v Persons Unknown (BAILII, EWHC 2628, 2015).

Case study

Brett Wilson, a firm of solicitors, was defamed on a website called Solicitors from Hell. The solicitors produced little evidence of 'serious financial loss' other than that of one client withdrawing their custom, and the fact that the offending article appeared within the top five on Google searches for six months. However, the court accepted this as sufficient proof; it did not require more substantial proof, such as company accounts.

THREE TYPES OF DEFAMATION

Defamation law in England and Wales is separated into three areas:

1. **Libel:** an allegation published in written or permanent form. This includes webpages, email messages, faxes, and radio and TV broadcasts. In the online environment, a libellous statement could be published as a:

   a. Tweet and Retweet or direct message.

   b. Facebook chat, wall post or direct message.

   c. Blog post or online article.

   d. Post on a message board or forum.

   e. A video or audio recording.

2. **Slander:** an allegation made in a transitory, non-permanent form, such as speech. Slander cases are rare.

3. **Malicious falsehood:** an allegation that falls short of damaging someone's reputation but is still harmful. For instance, it would not be defamatory to say that a famous singer had cancelled a concert because she had pneumonia. However, if the statement was false it could affect her earnings. She could sue if the publisher knew it was false or had not bothered to check the facts.

Libel is the most common form of defamation, partially because claimants must prove financial loss in cases of slander and malicious falsehood.

WHAT A LIBEL CLAIMANT MUST PROVE

A claimant must prove three things to succeed in a libel action:

1. **Defamation:** that the words defamed them. This means that 'a reasonable person' would believe that on the balance of probabilities, the words caused or were likely to cause them serious harm.

2. **Identification**: that the words referred to them. The test for identification is to whom the reasonable person or a friend of the claimant (someone who knows them already), would assume the words referred. There is no safety in not naming someone, giving clues to who they are, or using nicknames. In fact, vague identification or non-identification can be more dangerous, as this can allow other people with similar details to bring libel actions.

It is also possible to libel identifiable groups of people. For example, saying that 'architecture lecturers at Banshaw University have been fiddling students' exam grades' means that all the lecturers in that department could sue, even though none of them have been named. However, class actions are unlikely to succeed if the group exceeds more than about 12 to 15 people.

The internet has created a situation where it is possible to libel someone without naming them, or identifying them at all.

Case study

Former Chelsea and England defender Ashley Cole was the first person to claim 'jigsaw identification' in a libel case. In 2006, the News of the World (NoW) ran a story headlined "Gay as you Go". It alleged that two Premiership footballers, one capped several times for England, and a music industry figure were caught on camera involved in a "homosexual orgy" (Pink News, 2006, *Ashley Cole files lawsuit over gay orgy story*).

A week later, the newspaper published a heavily obscured photograph of two of the men allegedly involved, with the caption "Music Figure A and Player A." Some bloggers and websites later tracked down what they believed to be the original, unobscured image, which showed Cole together with a dance music DJ.

Cole sued the NoW and won the landmark legal argument that he became identified as one of the footballers in their allegations, when their article was read alongside material on the web. It was sufficient for Cole to say: "Everyone thinks it's me" (The Guardian, 2006, *England footballer sues tabloids*).

Case study

In February 2013, the High Court in Belfast awarded libel damages against an unidentified anonymous individual who posted abusive comments about two directors and a member of staff at a Belfast company. The individual, if ever identified, will have to pay damages of £35,000.

---

3. **Publication:** that the words were published to at least one third-party. Publication triggers a libel action, and every fresh publication can be treated as a new, separate libel action. It is not safe for someone to

claim that they are merely repeating a libellous statement made by someone else. If they publish it, they are legally responsible for it.

However, web editors who republish their own articles are protected by the DA 2013 if they:

a. Provide a new link to their own archived story.

b. Repeat one of their old broadcasts.

c. Republish an old article because new developments have made it current again.

d. Repeat the link or the story via Twitter, email or other social media.

e. Publish the article in a new edition of a book.

The DA only covers publishers who republish something they have previously published, provided it is not significantly different to the original. It does not protect someone else who publishes the offending material for the first time.

What is The Time Limit?

Libel actions must be started within 12 months of the date of first publication. In the online environment, this starts when an article is first published online, and is not considered a new publication each time an article is viewed or downloaded.

Where Can a Libel Claimant Start an Action?

Libel tourism used to be a problem in England and Wales because people from overseas took advantage of the strict libel laws and started actions for allegations made on websites in other countries. They claimed that it was acceptable to use the court in London because the defamatory statements could be viewed in the UK. However, the DA 2013 tightened this loophole. Now, someone from outside Europe cannot bring a libel case in London unless they can prove that England is the most appropriate place for it to be heard, and that they have a reputation to defend in England.

Libel tourism has only been considered in one court case under the DA 2013 so far (BAILII, EWHC 3380, 2015).

Mr Justice Tugendhat used it to lay out criteria for when the court will accept cases in England and Wales. Courts will consider:

1. The proportion of times that the article was published in England and Wales as opposed to elsewhere.

2. The amount of damage to the claimant's reputation in England and Wales compared with elsewhere.

3. The extent to which the publication was targeted at a readership in England and Wales compared with elsewhere.

4. Whether there was reason to think that the claimant would not receive a fair hearing elsewhere.

5. The convenience of witnesses and the relative expense of suing in different jurisdictions.

THE KEY QUESTION ON LIBEL

The key issue for web publishers is not whether people **can** sue, but whether they **will** sue. Publishers will usually weigh up the likelihood of a libel action when deciding whether to publish a contentious story. For example, one editor used to get his accounts department to do a credit check on possible libel claimants to see if they could afford to start proceedings!

Why people start libel actions

1. To clear their names.
2. To scare off other media and take control of the story.
3. To make money.
4. Because not acting will make them look guilty.
5. To discourage the media from publishing negative stories about them in future.

Why people do not start libel actions

1. They cannot afford to.
2. They are untroubled by the allegations; some people revel in the notoriety.
3. The claim is true.
4. They fear a publisher may produce unsavoury evidence about them as part of their defence in a court case.
5. The risk of perjury: if a claimant denies a truthful allegation under oath, they could face criminal prosecution. This is what happened to the former MP Jonathan Aitken (The Guardian, 1999, *Aitken jailed for 18 months*).
6. They do not want the publicity and resulting pressure.

THE DANGERS OF EMAIL

It is possible to libel someone in an email message if it is sent to more than one person – even by mistake. Journalists should check that they do not enter email addresses of those who should not receive the email, by accident.

This can happen with autocomplete and the "reply to all" options. This could be a problem if, for example, a journalist was emailing allegations to someone for their comment.

Journalists should also check emails before they forward them to other people, and make sure they delete any earlier conversations.

Case study

The danger of libelling someone in an email message was illustrated in January 2015 when a prominent member of the British Hindu community was awarded £45,000 in damages over two defamatory messages.

Hindu priest Pandit Dr Raj Sharma emailed defamatory allegations about Satish Sharma, general secretary of the National Council of Hindu Temples UK, in April 2013. The messages were sent to several Hindu temples, MPs and Lords.

Judge Moloney QC described the allegations as "poison" and said that the email messages percolated way beyond the initial recipients (CMP, 2016, *Sharma v Sharma EWHC 3349, 2014*).

LIBEL DEFENCES

Several defences are available to the online publisher, as well as arrangements for User Generated Content (UGC), which will be discussed later in this chapter. The defences are listed below.

Truth

Publishers will win libel cases if they can prove the "essential" or "substantial" truth of the offending words. This is more difficult than it sounds. In order to establish that an allegation is substantially true, a publisher may have to provide conclusive evidence, such as witness statements, photographs, documents and reports.

There is a big difference between believing an allegation is true and being able to prove it, on the balance of probability.

Honest opinion

This defence applies to:

1. Criticisms.

2. Observations.

3. Remarks.

Honest opinion is a generous defence because it is acceptable to express strong, malicious, spiteful and hurtful views about someone, provided the words are:

1. **Recognisable as comment**. Prefacing a statement with "in my opinion" does not mean that it qualifies as a comment.

For example, this is not a comment:

Premier League referee Mario Broccoli is not qualified to take charge of top-of-the-table clashes.

Why? Because it suggests he has not passed the relevant refereeing exams – a factual allegation.

This statement, however, would count as comment:

Premier League referee Mario Broccoli is useless – the worse referee to ever walk onto a football pitch. He should retire.

It can be hard distinguishing between a comment and a statement of fact. The simplest test is that a fact can be proved to be true or false, whereas a comment cannot be. However, even the courts sometimes find it difficult to separate the two.

2. **An honestly held view**. What the writer genuinely believed.

3. **Based on true facts.** This means that the writer should provide the background facts upon which the comment is based, even in general terms.

For example, this statement where the writer is commenting on a long-running public issue would probably be safe:

The city council's plan to cut social services spending is disgraceful. *Social services director, Jack Smith, should hang his head in shame. He is an insult to his profession.*

The words marked in **bold** indicate the facts on which the writer is commenting.

Privilege

There are certain occasions when the media must be able to publish defamatory content without fear of being sued. For instance, it would be dangerous for journalists to report court cases or ill-tempered council meetings if their publications could be sued for doing so. To enable reporting, these occasions are termed "privileged."

There are two types of privilege:

1. **Absolute privilege**. Under the DA 1996 absolute privilege protects media reports of court cases, provided they are fair, accurate, and published contemporaneously of the proceedings held in public.

2. **Qualified privilege.** Under the DA 1952, DA 1996 and DA 2013, qualified privilege protects reports based on:

    a. Council meetings.

    b. Official statements made on behalf of organisations such local authorities, the police and government departments, and disciplinary findings by governing bodies.

    c. Reports of public meetings and press conferences.

    d. Peer-reviewed statements in scientific and academic journals.

    e. Reports of scientific and academic conferences and related documents.

    f. Articles based on information provided by public companies.

g. Reports of proceedings of government, international conferences and international court proceedings, anywhere in the world.

To ensure qualified privilege, a report must be fair, accurate, on a matter of public concern or benefit, and published without malice. Some of the above are also subject to publication on request of a reasonable letter or statement of explanation or contradiction, sometimes referred to as the "right of reply".

Central and local government bodies frequently publish press releases about court cases that they have prosecuted, using the protection of qualified privilege.

However, some press offices are content to publish press releases that are unbalanced and one-sided, and which contain additional quotes without indicating that they were not part of the court proceedings – a practice that carries its own legal risks.

Some experts take the view that these "press releases" may actually count as "court reports" under the DA and should therefore be balanced.

Section 1 of the DA says that absolute and qualified privilege protects the "author" of a court report. But the author does not have to be a journalist. It could be a central or local government media team.

It can also be argued that media teams fulfil the function of "editors" under DA, because they have "[…] editorial or equivalent responsibility for the content of the statement or the decision to publish it" (GOV.UK, 2013, *Defamation Act*).

Tim Crook, Professor in Media and Communications at Goldsmiths, University of London, believes government press officers risk claims of malice if their press releases are excessively biased and one-sided, as occurred in the case Lillie & Anor v Newcastle City Council & Ors. Mr Justice Eady found malice in a council media release and awarded the claimants £200,000 each (BAILII, EWHC 1600(2), 2002).

Prof Crook said: "Privilege can break down as a defence if malice is proved, and if the fairness and accuracy of the reporting / representation is invalidated.

"Public authorities need to be very careful about media releases from court proceedings and legal matters. If malice is proved their qualified privilege crumbles.

"The demise of qualified and experienced court reporters means that so much online journalism is dependent on public authorities publishing media releases on the outcome of court cases.

"Their accounts would, in my opinion, be entitled to qualified privilege, and mainstream professional media publishers should always attribute and source this coverage with caution" (Press Gazette, 2016, *When government press officers think they are court reporters justice could be the loser*).

Some will say that this practice of publishing one-sided court reports seems to go against natural justice. People prosecuted by a government body may not receive balanced media coverage unless there's a "real" journalist in court.

It also invites the question: why do government media teams, who so frequently complain about press bias, choose not to cover both sides of a story, especially when there is a legal argument for doing so? Many experts would take the view that a court report is too important to be subjected to the "spin" process.

Public interest

Under the DA 2013, the public interest defence can be used if a publisher has a "reasonable belief" that publishing a defamatory allegation is in the public interest. Publishers will have to demonstrate that the copy was balanced and neutral and that thorough steps were taken to verify the facts.

The DA 2013's explanatory notes say that this defence is intended to reflect the common law as set out in Flood v Times Newspapers (2012) in which Lord Mance stated that it would seldom be in the public interest "[…] to publish material which has not been the subject of responsible journalistic enquiry and consideration […]"(BAILII, UKSC 11, 2012).

The case of Economou v de Freitas was the first case to look at the defence in detail clarifying that the court will place a great deal of weight on whether the defendant "reasonably believed" the publication was in the public interest and not just on whether it was a general matter of public interest (Courts and Tribunals Judiciary, 2016, *Economou v de Freitas [2016] EWHC 1853 (QB)*).

The defendant (D) was the father of the late Eleanor de Freitas. In December 2012, Ms de Freitas and the claimant (C) had a relationship. She accused him of rape the following year, and C was later arrested and charged. Ms de Freitas denied the charge and committed suicide four days before the trial date.

D wanted the subsequent inquest to examine the Crown Prosecution Service's role in this. The coroner initially ruled against this, and D was advised by his solicitor to go public with a series of media statements and broadcasts, which he did in November and December 2014.

C then sued The Guardian, BBC Radio 4 Today, The Daily Telegraph and The Guardian for libel.

D successfully used the public interest defence, with Mr Justice Warby saying that the defence depended on the specific circumstances of each case. In this case, there was a distinction between the defendant, as the father who had lost a child, and a journalist, whose reasons for pursuing publication would be different.

HOW TO PROTECT COPY FROM LIBEL

Journalists should always:

1. Check their facts and only write statements where the meaning is clear, and that can be proved to be true, with solid, reliable evidence. Take care that words used for effect in headlines and intros are supported by evidence – for example, the word "deliberate". Inferences and barbed remarks must be proved as well.

2. Check that sources are credible and willing to appear as witnesses in a libel trial.

3. Corroborate allegations; single-source stories should be treated with caution.

4. Exercise sufficient care and judgment in researching, compiling and presenting their stories. Mention what information they do not know so that readers understand the broader picture.

5. Avoid words that deal with motives, for example, "misleading".

6. Check which defence the claimant would use should the case come to court, and make sure they can comply with the conditions.

LIBEL ON TWITTER (TWIBEL)

It is safe to Tweet or Retweet comments if they fulfil the conditions of the honest opinion defence, outlined above. However, Tweets or Retweets can be defamatory if they contain a factual allegation that causes, or is likely to cause, serious harm to someone's reputation.

Case study

The best example of a Twibel was the case of Lord McAlpine v Sally Bercow (Carruthers Law, 2013, *Lord McAlpine of West Green v Sally Bercow*). Bercow posted a Tweet saying: "Why is Lord McAlpine trending? *Innocent face*" two days after a Newsnight report that wrongly implicated the former Conservative party treasurer in allegations of historic sex abuse. McAlpine said it pointed the finger of blame, and he won undisclosed damages.

Bercow did not actually make an allegation against the peer. She just made a pointed suggestion that was seen as libel by innuendo (it contained a hidden meaning).

Case study

In the case, Peter Cruddas v Mark Adams, MP Cruddas won £45,000 in libel damages for a persistent and public Twitter campaign alleging he was a criminal who flouted electoral law (BAILII, EWHC 145, 2013).

How to make Tweets and Retweets safe from libel

Journalists should:

1. Check for hidden meanings.

2. Check the facts can be proved – even in Retweets.

3. Take care with hashtags. For example, this is safe (if it is true):

    BBC reports that England star Barry Briggs was stopped for speeding.

    But, these hashtags make the statement potentially defamatory:

    BBC reports that England star Barry Briggs was stopped for speeding #dangerous #driver #criminal.

LIBEL ON FACEBOOK

It is also possible to libel someone on Facebook. Statements allegedly posted to a private Facebook account have already resulted in one High Court judgment.

Case study

Joanne Walder accused a woman named Sharon Smith of posting statements that alleged that she had engaged in criminal acts of violence. Ms Walder said the statements were false and unfounded, and won the case.

The judgment was the first successful claim of its kind that dealt with status updates posted on a private profile. They were visible only to Ms Smith's 300 "friends", but Ms Smith's sister copied the comments to her wall, so they were then visible to at least 650 "friends".

But, the sister's profile was also public, which meant that the allegations could, in theory, be read by anyone. Ms Smith was therefore held liable for posting the comments herself, and for the further publication to "a significant but unknown number of persons" (Schillings, 2014, *Landmark Facebook libel case*).

Case study

Media websites would do well to heed a decision by the Northern Ireland High Court about the way Facebook responded to a take-down request.

The case involved a convicted sex offender – known as CG – who settled in a town in Northern Ireland after being released from prison.

A Facebook user published details about him on a public page under the heading "Keeping our Kids Safe from Predators 2." They included his identity, details of his family and his previous criminal convictions, and several threats.

The man's solicitors contacted Facebook and asked it to remove the post. Facebook finally took it down three weeks later. During that time, it attracted several Likes and a string of insults and threatening comments from Facebook users.

In the High Court, the social media site defended its actions using the EU ECD Regulations 2002. This is the law that gives media websites immunity from prosecutions over unmoderated illegal comments on their message boards.

Facebook said it was not obliged to take down the post because CG's solicitors did not provide the offending post's URL, or sufficient details about it. It quoted a regulation which absolves the site from liability if they "[…] did not have actual knowledge of unlawful activity or information."

But the High Court rejected Facebook's argument. It ruled that Facebook had sufficient information to realise that the post was unlawful.

Mr Justice Girvan said: "The only efficacious remedy was to remove all the postings. [...] Facebook has considerable resources at its disposal and does not require to have spelled out to it on each occasion with inappropriate precision the particular laws of the UK which are in issue and which are being contravened" (Courts NI, 2015, *Court awards damages against Joseph McCloskey and Facebook for identifying sex offender: Summary of Judgment*).

He added: "It can also be assumed that the first defendant knows that harassing and threatening violence against sex offenders together with attempts to publicise exactly where the sex offender lives are also unlawful being the misuse of private information and contrary to public policy" (Courts NI, 2015, *CG v Facebook Ireland Ltd. [2015] NIQB 11*).

The lesson for media which run unmoderated message boards is clear. Yes, they have immunity from prosecution under the European Union (EU) Regulations. But that immunity may fail if they do not respond quickly to take-down requests about posts that involve breaches of the law.

LIBEL ON MESSAGE BOARDS

Three laws provide publishers with defences for legal actions resulting from posts on their message boards:

1. EU ECD Regulations 2002.
2. DA 1996: innocent dissemination.

3. DA 2013: section 5 defence. This act requires a lot of complex administration, and it is hard to see why a webmaster would use it.

These laws are alike and state that online publishers are not responsible for online visitors' posts, if:

1. **They do not moderate the content**: their message boards are just a means of storing and passing on information, and are not edited. The following actions can be interpreted as editing:

   a. Manually updating entries on a homepage's auto-generated lists of blogs and recommended blogs.

   b. Correcting spelling and grammar.

   c. Controlling quality.

   d. Deleting spam.

   e. Deleting obscenity, bad language, etc.

2. **They operate a "report and remove" system** and take-down offensive posts quickly if they receive a complaint.

The ECtHR has also examined the publication of readers' comments.

Case study

In the case Magyar Tartalomszolgaltatok Egyesulete and Index.Hu Zrt V. Hungary, the ECtHR ruled, in February 2016, that making websites responsible for the content of the comments section would breach freedom of expression rights.

The case involved a Hungarian website that was sued for messages on its forum about a company. The comments were removed as soon as they were reported.

Defence lawyers said there would be serious repercussions on freedom of expression if their clients were liable for everything readers posted. The judges agreed, and ruled that Hungarian courts were wrong to rule in favour of the unnamed company.

They said in their judgment: "Although offensive and vulgar, the incriminated comments did not constitute clearly unlawful speech; and they certainly did not amount to hate speech or incitement to violence" (BAILII, ECHR 135, 2016).

Case study

The system of "report and remove" was thrown into some doubt by a surprising decision by the ECtHR. The case involved the large Estonian news website, Delfi, in 2015.

In January 2006, Delfi published a story about a ferry company's controversial decision to change its routes. The article attracted more than 180 comments, including 20 that threatened and abused the ferry company's majority shareholder. The comments bypassed Delfi's automatic "bad language" filtering system.

The ferry company sued for libel and won both its case and an appeal under Estonian libel law, even though Delfi removed the comments quickly after receiving a complaint. Delfi took the case to the ECtHR, claiming the Estonian courts breached their rights of freedom of expression.

However, the court found in favour of the ferry company's majority shareholder, and Delfi was fined 320 euros.

The judges said: "By publishing the article in question, [Delfi] could have realised that it might cause negative reactions against the shipping company and its managers and that, considering the general reputation of comments on the Delfi news portal, there was a higher-than-average risk that the negative comments could go beyond the boundaries of acceptable criticism and reach the level of gratuitous insult or hate speech" (BAILII, ECHR 941, 2013).

This ruling appeared to contradict the ECD, and showed that there are some circumstances when "report and remove" cannot be relied upon.

Delfi appealed the decision and, in June 2015, the Grand Chamber of the European Court supported the ECtHR's earlier decision by a majority of 15-2. It agreed that Delfi was liable for making the "grossly insulting" comments available on its website, and that the company exercised a substantial degree of control over its news portal.

The judges said that Delfi's role went beyond that of a passive, purely technical service provider (BAILII, ECHR 586, 2015).

Although this ruling seems to contradict that of the case above, it should be remembered that the comments on the Delfi site amounted to hate speech.

It remains to be seen what effect the ruling, and the appeal, will have on UK websites. UK courts are not legally bound by ECtHR decisions. They must only "take them into account". However, they generally attempt to make judgments that are compatible with the convention.

The ruling has added to the uncertainty as to how the ECtHR relates to the ECD at a time when the European Commission is reviewing the directive in a consultation that commenced in September 2015 (see section below).

CONCERNS ABOUT THE FUTURE OF THE ECD

The European Commission (EC) launched a consultation in 2015 about the development of a digital single market, including the regulatory framework currently provided by the ECD.

The consultation followed publication of the EC's report titled "A Digital Single Market Strategy for Europe" (European Commission, 2016, *A Digital Single Market Strategy for Europe*).

The report floated the need for new measures to tackle illegal internet content, and "rigorous" procedures for removing it, including "[…] whether to require intermediaries to exercise greater responsibility and due diligence in the way they manage their networks and systems – a duty of care."

The consultation concluded in December 2015. The preliminary findings can be seen here: https://ec.europa.eu/digital-single-market/en/news/summary-report-public-consultation-evaluation-and-review-regulatory-framework-electronic (European Commission, 2016, *A Digital Single Market*).

The EC will be publishing a final report in due course.

However, if it recommends that website operators have a duty of care over their content, then the days of unmoderated contributions and the "report and remove" system could soon be over.

CONTEMPT OF COURT

Journalists can face criminal prosecution if they seriously prejudice someone's trial by publishing something that could influence a jury.

Case study

In March 2014, GQ magazine published an article by journalist Michael Wolff, headlined "The court without a king" during the phone hacking trial of former NoW employees Andy Coulson and Rebekah Brooks.

The article was prejudicial to the trial of Brooks and Coulson because the jury could have got the impression after reading the article that the "newspaper's owner, Rupert Murdoch, or his senior staff had either directed or known about phone hacking and had a 'hidden agenda' at the trial" (The Guardian, 2015, *GQ article*).

The trial judge, Mr Justice Saunders, agreed that the article appeared to be a contempt of court, and around 100,000 copies of the magazine were taken off the shelves.

The magazine's owners, Condé Nast Publications, were found guilty of contempt in November 2015 and fined £10,000 plus nearly £50,000 costs (BAILII, EWHC 3322, 2015).

Case study

In 2012, while the jury was considering its verdict in the case of the alleged abduction of a teenage girl (Rachel Cowles), the Daily Mirror and the Daily Mail published an allegation that the defendant, Levi Bellfield, had a sexual interest in young girls.

The newspapers published the allegation after a jury had found Bellfield guilty of the kidnap and murder of teenager Milly Dowler, but before it had reached a verdict in relation to the kidnap attempt on Rachel.

The court fined the newspapers for publishing prejudicial material. This contempt of court was so serious that the jury was discharged (BAILII, EWHC 2981, 2012).

The Contempt of Court Act (CCA) 1981's strict liability rule says that any publication that creates a substantial risk of serious prejudice or impediment to the administration of justice may be treated as contempt, regardless of intent, if proceedings are active. "Active" usually covers the period from someone's arrest to the conclusion of their trial (CPS, 2009, *Contempt of Court and Reporting Restrictions: Strict Liability Contempt under the Contempt of Court Act 1981*).

Any writing, speech, broadcast or other communication can be in contempt, so the public faces the same dangers as journalists do. Dominic Grieve, as Attorney General, said he would prosecute publishers of social media remarks that breached the law. Legal warnings are posted on the Attorney General's Twitter feed @attorneygeneral, and its website.

The risks of prejudice increase if:

1. A trial is less than six months away; the nearer it gets, the greater the risk.

2. It is a high-profile or memorable case that sticks in jurors' minds.

3. A trial is in progress.

CONTENT THAT CAN CREATE PREJUDICE

The main dangers are:

1. Saying that the person who was arrested is the same person who committed the crime, or using details implying that he is, for example: "The suspect was arrested carrying a sawn-off shotgun."

2. Commenting on the credibility of witnesses or their evidence.

3. Saying why a defendant might be guilty or innocent.

4. Revealing a defendant's previous convictions or even their acquittals.

5. Mentioning details of a defendant's lifestyle, character, or previous court appearances.

6. Publishing descriptions or photographs of the defendant, especially if they are basing their defence on mistaken identity.

    This applies unless these are used as part of a police appeal to apprehend a suspected criminal. However, these should not continue to be used once a defendant has been arrested.

7. Disclosing information that the jury has not yet heard.

8. Publishing links to pre-trial stories.

9. Mentioning cases involving a defendant.

The Attorney General, the police, or counsel involved in the case can ask webmasters to remove online material that could create prejudice. They can also apply to the court for a CCA section 4 order to delay publication of prejudicial material until a date set by the court. See the section Defences, below.

Case study

In February 2016, the Court of Appeal made an order, under section 45(4) of the Senior Courts Act 1981, against a group of nine media organisations forbidding them to publish reports of a trial on their Facebook Profiles and Pages, and they were told to disable their website message boards.

The trial was of a case of two girls charged with the murder of Angela Wrightson, 39, who was battered to death in her home in Hartlepool in December, 2014. A previous trial of this case was halted at Teesside Crown Court in July 2015 following a wave of comment and abuse on social media.

Editors were warned that they may face prosecution under the CCA if they did not comply with the order. This was the first time the Court of Appeal issued a specific ban on social media to avoid comments prejudicing a trial.

In a similar move in April 2016, media organisations covering the trial of two women accused of murdering a two-year-old were asked not to publish stories on social media, and to disable their message boards.

The Scottish Courts and Tribunals Service made the request because potentially prejudicial comments were being posted under reports of the trial of Nyomi Fee, 28, and Rachel Fee, 31, for the murder of Rachel's son Liam in a house near Glenrothes in March 2014 (Society of Editors, 2016, *New alert over internet comment contempt risk*).

Archived material is usually safe, provided the website does not provide a new link to it, draw attention to it, or republish it. However, web editors need to make sure that automatic tools do not produce unwanted links to active cases.

Web editors should avoid allowing people to comment on crimes or court cases once proceedings are active.

Case study

In summer 2016, the newspaper St Helen's Star, Lancashire, asked readers to refrain from commenting on a Facebook social signal (Facebook, 2016, *Campaigner tells court she did not provoke alleged kick*) about an ongoing court case involving local MP Marie Rimmer.

However, the newspaper's followers quickly weighed in with comments ranging from the MP being as "guilty as hell" to "Marie didn't do anything wrong."

One follower probably struck a more helpful note by stating: "Why not just turn the option off to post comments then?"

Ms Rimmer was later acquitted of kicking a Yes campaigner outside a polling station on the day of the Scottish independence referendum.

OTHER CONTEMPT OF COURT RISKS

Journalists can also commit contempt of court by:

1. Naming or identifying jurors.

2. Disclosing, obtaining or soliciting information about statements made, opinions expressed, arguments advanced or votes cast by members of a jury.

These actions are crimes under section 74 of the Criminal Justice and Courts Act 2015. A journalist could be jailed for up to two years, or given an unlimited fine, if convicted (UK Legislation, n.d., *Criminal Justice and Courts Act 2015*).

3.   Breaching a court injunction. Some people's identities
     are protected by a lifelong injunction.

Case study

The best-known example is Maxine Carr who
provided a false alibi for her boyfriend Ian Huntley
after he murdered Holly Wells and Jessica Chapman,
in Soham, Cambridgeshire in 2002.

Case study

Another well-known example is the case of Robert
Thompson and Jon Venables who, as children, were
convicted of murdering James Bulger.

In 2013, the police served injunctions on Google,
Twitter and Facebook, ordering them to remove
photographs supposedly showing these convicts as
they look as adults. The Attorney General warned that
he would prosecute anyone who published the images
(The Guardian, 2013, *Google, Facebook and Twitter ordered
to delete photos of James Bulger killers*).

Case study

In December 2016, the High Court passed a similar
lifelong injunction on two brothers who tortured two
other children in South Yorkshire when they were
aged 10 and 11.

They were originally granted anonymity until the age
of 18, in 2010. The High Court has now extended the
anonymity because they would be at serious risk of
attack.

ONLINE LAW FOR JOURNALISTS

> The boys lured their victims to a ravine and carried out a "sadistic" attack in Edlington, near Doncaster, in 2009 (BBC News, 2010, *Edlington attack "could have been prevented"*).

DEFENCES

The CCA provides three defences:

1. **Innocent publication**. Under section 3 of the CCA, journalists may have the defence of innocent publication if they can prove that having taken all reasonable care, they did not know and had no reason to believe that proceedings were active.

    This means that journalists must check if proceedings are active in a case, which may involve checking with the police (or press officer) and with the court. Details of the time and date of the call, the name of the officer or official spoken to and the nature of their reply should be noted in writing.

2. **Contemporary reports of proceedings**. Under the section 4 defence of the CCA the media will not be liable for publishing a court report that prejudices another case, provided the report is:

    a. Fair.

    b. Accurate.

    c. Published contemporaneously.

    d. Published in good faith.

    However, the judge may override the section 4 defence by passing a section 4 order, as mentioned above, which will delay the publication of a report of a case (or some other material, like a photo) until a given date.

When judges pass the section 4 order, they must state:

    a. Why it was passed.

    b. The evidence it applies to.

    c. When it expires.

3. **Discussion in good faith of public affairs**. The CCA's section 5 defence allows the media to publish background stories about issues arising from a court case, but not the case itself, while proceedings are active, provided they are in the public interest and the risk of prejudice is incidental to the discussion.

For example, if a teenager is arrested today for stabbing a fellow pupil at school, proceedings will be active. However, it would be safe for the media to publish stories (accompanying the newsbreak), on subjects such as security in schools and the availability of knives on the internet.

PROTECTING PEOPLE'S IDENTITIES

Web editors and journalists can be prosecuted for contempt of court if they publish content or images that identify someone who is legally protected, such as:

1. Alleged victims of any sexual offence, or victims of Female Genital Mutilation (FGM).

2. Under-18s involved in crime, either as suspects, defendants, witnesses or victims.

3. Teachers accused of offences against pupils at their schools.

4. Under-18s, and certain adults, involved in ward of court or family court cases.

The law is applied strictly. People with protected identities must remain anonymous, even to people who know them, including parents, partners, husbands, wives, close family members or work colleagues.

The more details that are used, the more dangerous it is, especially when facts are used together with a person's age. Ages are best generalised.

It is also important to check which details other media have used, to avoid the "jigsaw effect". Web editors should just use the same details that other media have used, and not add any other facts.

Media organisations should make sure they use the same details in items appearing on their printed, web, and social media platforms.

If an online visitor reveals someone's identity on an unmoderated media website, the web editor may be safe from prosecution under the EU ECD.

Risks with photographs

Photographs should be checked even if they have been pixelated, because they might include identifying features such as hairstyles, hats or clothes and tattoos. A location can also provide clues so these must be checked. Photographs of people facing away from the camera or taken from behind should also be checked in case they lead to identification.

Case study

In March 2016, ex-Sun newspaper editor David Dinsmore was ordered to pay £2,300 for breaching the Sexual Offences (Amendment) Act 1992 for publishing a photograph of a sexual offence victim.

The Sun printed a Facebook photograph of a teenage girl who had fallen victim to former AFC Sunderland player, Adam Johnson, who was subsequently jailed for grooming and sexual activity with a child.

The newspaper took extensive steps to obscure the girl's identity: it replaced the background, changed the girl's clothing, the length and colour of her hair, and substituted her head with an oval white shape.

However, Westminster Magistrates Court ruled that people who had seen the Facebook page would realise that the Sun had used the same image. They used the strict legal test: could she be identified as a victim by people who knew her?

The Sun had mistakenly used a lower threshold: could she be identified by the average man and woman in the street? This was surprising as the stricter test had been widely used for many years. The case indicates the lengths the courts will go to safeguard people whose identities are legally protected.

Risks with written content

Facts that can lead to identification must be removed, especially when used with a location such as the name of a village or small geographical area, or a geotag that includes a postcode.

Other facts that need to be checked are listed below.

Unusual facts about a person

For example:

1. She has eight brothers and sisters.

2. He rides a quad bike.

3. Her mother is a ballet teacher.

4. She was out walking her two Dalmatians.

The circumstances of a crime

For example:

1. She was on her way home from her French evening class.

2. It happened in Victoria Park, just after the under-12s cup final.

3. He was following his usual journey to work after catching the 8.10am from London Bridge.

Specific details of injuries sustained in an attack

For example:

1. She received 50 stitches to a facial wound.

2. He is now on crutches.

3. Her hands were seriously burned in the attack.

Cases involving people from the same family

These must be treated with extreme care; for instance, if a father is accused of indecently assaulting his child.

Clause 7(2) of the Independent Press Standards Organisation's (Ipso) Editors' Code of Practice specifies that:

1. The child must not be identified.

2. The adult may be identified.

3. The word "incest" must not be used where a child victim might be identified.

4. Care must be taken that nothing in the report implies the relationship between the accused and the child.

The fourth condition means that many significant details of the case must be omitted.

When anonymity applies

Listed below are the main circumstances when anonymity applies.

Alleged sexual offences

The Sexual Offences Act 2003, when taken with the Sexual Offences Act 1976, and the Criminal Justice Act 1988 says that a complainant of any sexual offence may not be identified as an alleged victim, in their lifetime, from the moment of complaint. The Youth Justice and Criminal Evidence Act (YJCEA) 1999 forbids the use of:

1.   Their name, address, school, college or workplace.

2.   Any particulars leading to their identification.

3.   Any photograph of or including them.

Under-18s involved in crime

Most court cases involving under-18s are dealt with in youth courts. However, some young people are tried in an adult magistrate's court or the crown court if they are charged with serious offences, or are jointly charged with an adult.

When a child or young person appears in a youth court, either as a defendant, witness or a victim, the Children and Young Persons Act 1933 and YJCEA 1999 jointly forbid the reporting of the same details listed in point 1, above.

On conviction, the media can apply for the restrictions to be lifted in the public interest, under the Crime (Sentences) Act 1997.

Case study

In April 2016, Mr Justice Globe refused to allow the media to name the two teenage girls convicted for the brutal murder of Angela Wrightson.

He accepted arguments made by media organisations that there was legitimate public interest in naming the girls, now 15. However, he said that the girls' welfare was at risk.

He said: "They (defence barristers) emphasise the fact that each defendant poses a risk of self-harm. In one case, it is a real and present danger. Removing anonymity is likely to exacerbate what is already a dangerous situation" (Hold the Front Page, 2016, *Wrightson judge explains why he kept killers' names secret*).

He added that if the girls were "stable, strong-minded defendants", the balance might have been in favour of lifting the anonymity.

The restrictions can also be lifted by the home secretary, under the Children and Young Persons Act 1969, to avoid injustice to a juvenile, and by the director of public prosecutions who may apply for the lifting under the Criminal Justice and Public Order Act 1994, to trace a juvenile wanted for a violent or sexual offence or any offence for which an adult could be jailed for 14 years or more.

If under-18s appears in an adult court, they can be named unless the court passes a section 45 order under the YJCEA. The order can be passed on witnesses, victims and defendants, and the anonymity requirements are the same as above.

These are the key points about section 45 orders:

1. Any criminal court can pass the order on any under-18 victim, witness or defendant who is involved in the proceedings.

2. The order applies to print and broadcast media and online publications.

3. When deciding whether to pass the order, the court must have regard to the welfare of the child or young person.

4. If it is passed, a journalist cannot publish the child's name, address or school, college or workplace, or any particulars leading to their identification by people who know them; or any photograph of or including any such juvenile.

5. The court may remove or relax the section 45 reporting restriction if satisfied that it imposes a substantial and unreasonable restriction on reporting, and that it is in the public interest. This means the media can challenge the order on these grounds.

6. The order expires when the child or young person turns 18. But, a victim or witness may have their anonymity protected for the rest of their lives (see the next section).

7. The order cannot be passed just because the person is under-18. The court must balance the child's welfare against the public interest and the media's right to report.

The media can challenge an order by persuading the court that:

a. It imposes a substantial and unreasonable restriction on reporting.

b. It is in the public interest.

Section 45 orders expire when the young person turns 18, or when proceedings finish if they turn 18 during the case. Under-18 victims and witnesses can also be given lifelong anonymity in certain circumstances.

Teacher anonymity

Teachers accused of offences against children at their schools receive lifelong anonymity under the Education Act 2011, unless they are charged.

FGM victims

The media must not identity victims and alleged victims of FGM and related offences, once an allegation has been made. This provision comes under section 71 of the Serious Crime Act 2015, and also covers offences related to FGM.

Lifelong anonimity is also being introduced this year (2017) for victims and alleged victims of forced marriage.

Wards of court hearings and family law cases

Section 12 of the Administration of Justice Act, and the Children Act 1989, impose strict restrictions on reporting the hearings, and identifying people involved in the cases. It may not be possible to report them at all.

Scottish law falls into line with Europe

The age at which charged youths can be named in the Scottish media was raised from 16 to 18 last August, in a move to bring Scotland into line with the UK and the rest of Europe. Previously, anyone accused of a crime lost their anonymity at 16 as they were considered to be adults in Scots law.

Young offenders and accused people aged 16 and 17 can no longer be identified in Scottish criminal cases.

The change is part of the Victims and Witnesses (Scotland) Act 2014, and applies to defendants and witnesses.

Although the change was approved in 2014, it did not come into effect until 2015 and caught many journalists and lawyers by surprise. The Scottish government announced the implementation date in May 2015, but did not issue any reminders after that.

COURT REPORTING

Journalists may attend and report court cases, subject to a range of restrictions that can be downloaded here:

https://www.judiciary.gov.uk/publications/reporting-restrictions-in-the-criminal-courts-2/

It is contempt of court to make audio recordings of court proceedings, and the Criminal Justice Act 1925 makes it an offence to take or publish a photograph or sketch of parties or witnesses in the courtroom, or of people entering or leaving the court or its precincts.

The term "precincts" has never been defined, so this can cause uncertainty for journalists wanting to photograph people involved in court cases.

The safest option is to photograph them away from the court buildings, and to heed any instructions from police or court officials to move on.

Journalists should also make sure they do not take photographs of jurors or of people whose identities are legally protected. And web editors should check that these people are not inadvertently included in background shots.

TWEETING FROM COURT

The lord chief justice said in 2012 that journalists and legal commentators can cover court cases using Twitter or live blogging platforms, without consent.

Guidance is available on this downloadable PDF:
https://www.judiciary.gov.uk/wp-content/uploads/JCO/Documents/Guidance/ltbc-guidance-dec-2011.pdf

These reports, when taken together, must be a fair, balanced, and accurate summary. This can be challenging in a series of 140-character Tweets.

In cases where a defendant pleads not guilty, journalists should ensure that each day's Tweets:

1. Include the defendant's plea.

2. Do not present allegations as fact. Evidence must be frequently qualified with statements like: "The jury heard", or "It was alleged."

3. State that the case continues at the end of each day's proceedings.

Journalists are also advised to avoid using hashtags that can lead to other Tweets containing prejudicial material or restricted identities.

TAKING NOTES IN COURT

It is not unusual for judges and magistrates to challenge note-taking, or even ban it, as they did during the Operation Elveden trials, although this restriction only applied to people in the public gallery, not the press benches.

However, the position should change following a ruling by the Queen's Bench Division (QBD) of the High Court, discussed below.

The court ruled that anyone (press or public) can take notes without consent. However, a court can still ban note-taking, if there is a good reason.

Case study

The case, Ewing v Cardiff Crown Court, involved a man called Terence Ewing who was threatened with contempt after a judge spotted him taking notes in the public gallery during an appeal case in 2014.

Ewing appealed the ruling and won his argument.

The QBD judges, Lord Justice Burnett and Mr Justice Sweeney, said the judge in the original case was wrong. They referred to Her Majesty's Courts and Tribunals Service guidelines to staff, that say: "There can be no objection to note-taking in the public gallery unless it is done for a wrongful purpose; for example, to brief a witness who is not in court on what has already happened" (BAILII, EWHC 183, 2016).

They said that note-taking was different to live blogging, where members of the public need to get the court's consent in advance.

The QBD's ruling does not give the press any greater rights than members of the public. But it will be welcomed by journalists, especially when they have to sit in the public gallery because the press benches are full.

The ruling only applies to taking notes.

WEBSITE DISCLAIMERS, TERMS AND CONDITIONS

Media organisations should protect themselves and their online visitors by using disclaimers, and terms and conditions (T&Cs) on their websites.

A media website that allows comments and UGC should provide T&Cs that:

1. Inform visitors that their anonymity cannot be guaranteed, and that their details may be divulged to the courts if they post anything illegal.

2. Require visitors to register their names and contact details and accept the T&Cs by proactively ticking a box, before contributing to the site.

3. Explain that offensive posts may be removed if someone complains.

4. Provide a robust complaints policy and "report abuse" procedure.

COMPLAINTS PROCEDURES

Media websites should provide a complaints procedure, a "report abuse" button, and an email address or a form for users to use to make complaints.

If they plan to use the DA 2013's section 5 defence, they may need to institute two complaints procedures: one for defamatory comments and one for everything else, as the DA has unique procedures that might need to be explained separately.

Website operators should train someone to monitor complaints every day, and organise holiday, sickness and maternity cover to ensure continuity. An unacknowledged complaint could prove to be costly.

DISCLAIMERS

Online publishers are naive if they believe that publishing an all-embracing disclaimer can exonerate them from legal risks.

Anyone who communicates anything electronically may be held liable for breaching any number of laws.

This particularly affects both freelancers and news agencies that syndicate copy and images to a broad range of organisations. Thus, freelancers and news agencies should use a disclaimer something like this:

> While every effort is taken to ensure it is accurate and up to date, I, [Name], am not liable for any errors or inaccuracies in the copy.

> Images are subject to the copyright conditions stated at the top of the copy or embedded in the image metadata, and are distributed in good faith on the basis that the copyright information is correct.

> Media organisations who use copy or images provided by me accept that the decision to publish them is solely theirs, and that they are responsible for all legal and ethical outcomes arising from that decision.

> They should check that the copy and images conform to all relevant laws and regulatory codes, prior to publication or broadcast.

I will not accept liability for any expense, damage or loss that publishers may incur because of their decision to publish.

GETTING ONLINE CONTENT REMOVED

People who believe an item is damaging their career prospects, or causing them embarrassment may ask web editors to remove online content. There is no obligation to comply with these requests, and web editors should treat each request on its merits.

However, they should treat take-down requests from a solicitor, the police, or a government agency seriously.

THE RIGHT TO BE FORGOTTEN

Case study

In May 2014, the ECJ ruled, in the case Google Spain SL v Agencia Española de Protección de Datos, that EU citizens can request search engines to remove links to webpages that contain content that is inadequate, irrelevant, or excessive (5RB, n.d., *Google Spain SL v Agencia Española de Protección de Datos*).

Google has published criteria for deciding these "right to be forgotten" requests. The criteria can be viewed here: https://support.google.com/legal/answer/3110420?rd=2

The decision does not apply to online media archives, but this has not stopped people submitting take-down requests to national and local newspapers. The ICO has confirmed that media organisations must consider these requests. However, web editors can legitimately refuse them, using the journalistic exemption under section 32 of the DPA.

The ruling has made it harder for journalists to research stories. However, delisted content can sometimes be found via the Google cache facility. This can be accessed by searching for a website by name and selecting "cached" by clicking on the down arrow next to the website's address in the search results.

Delisted content can also be found by searching on Google.com, which targets searchers in America. The US's constitutional right to free speech gives Google the "right to remember".

In June 2015, The Guardian newspaper revealed that fewer than 5% of nearly 220,000 take-down requests submitted to Google concerned criminals, politicians and high-profile public figures (The Guardian, 2015, *Google accidentally reveals data on "right to be forgotten" requests*).

The findings tend to disprove the myth that most take-down requests come from criminals trying to conceal their dubious pasts. The Guardian obtained the figures by analysing archived versions of Google's transparency report.

However, the signs are that the "right to be forgotten" will soon be extended to all areas of online activity by the new EU GDPR, which is due to be introduced later this year (2016).

The regulation was agreed by the EC, Parliament and Council of Ministers in December, and was expected to be finally ratified by the European Parliament as *Online Law for Journalists* went to press.

The regulation will increase consumers' rights over their data. In future, for example, they may be able to ask a social media network to delete their profile completely – something that is not possible now.

The changes are unlikely to extend to media articles, as these should be protected by freedom of expression under the ECHR.

EU member states will have two years to implement the new regulation.

Case study

In December 2015, the "right to be forgotten" ruling was affirmed by the Court of Rome (Court of Rome, 3 December 2015, No. 23771, Dott.ssa Damiana Colla) in a very similar case to the original Google Spain ruling.

An Italian lawyer brought an action against Google to obtain an injunction order for the removal of 14 URLs which eventually came up in the search engine's results list every time he searched his own name.

They linked to webpages containing information on previous criminal cases in which he was allegedly involved between 2012 and 2013 (IPlens, 2016, *Right to be forgotten: the first Italian decision after Google Spain*).

HOW SOME MEDIA ARE UNDERMINING THE RULING

The Surrey Comet and other newspapers have undermined the ECJ ruling by running stories detailing an individual's "right to be forgotten" request to Google. This tactic brings the story back into the public eye and also produces a new Google hyperlink.

Case study

In September 2015, Google was served a "remove or else" order by the ICO over links to stories held in some online media archives.

It is the first public enforcement notice served by the ICO since the "right to be forgotten" was introduced by the ECJ in 2014. It is likely to affect links to content in media archives and the "public right to know".

The case involved an individual in the UK who asked Google to remove a link to a story in a newspaper's archive about their conviction for a minor offence ten years ago. Google complied, but the newspaper then published a story about the removal, including details of the original conviction, which was spent under the Rehabilitation of Offenders Act. Other media also published articles about it.

The individual then asked Google to remove the links to the new newspaper story, but they refused, saying they were relevant and published in the public interest. The individual then appealed to the ICO.

The ICO ruled against Google. According to David Smith, the ICO Deputy Commissioner, the individual was not involved in public life and that the story breached their privacy and was likely to cause them distress. He also noted that the original conviction was not current.

Smith added that the ICO accepted that the search results related to journalistic content and were both newsworthy and in the public interest. However, he said that the public interest could be served without doing a search using the complainant's name.

Google was given 35 days to remove the offending links or risk further enforcement action (ICO, 2015, *CO orders removal of Google search results*). It considered appealing, but eventually complied by changing the way it delists search results. The ICO told Online Law for Journalists that Google's new approach appeared to address its concerns (ICO, 2015, *Google Inc*).

Online Abuse

The law has been slow to respond to online abuse, and some people have behaved online in ways that would have resulted in arrest and punishment in the real world. However, prosecutions are becoming more common.

In 2013, the former director of public prosecutions Keir Starmer published guidelines for prosecutions involving online abuse, and warned that people will be prosecuted if they post messages that:

1. Make credible threats of violence.

2. Are targeted campaigns of harassment against an individual.

3. Breach court orders.

4. Are grossly offensive, indecent, obscene or false.

However, the guidelines say that the authorities should take a relaxed approach to banter, jokes and offensive messages, including:

1. Satire and jokes that are silly or made in bad taste.

2. Rudeness.

3. Unpopular or unfashionable opinions.

4. Distasteful and hurtful comments.

Under-18s and Tweeters with few followers are less likely to be prosecuted.

Social media online abuse guidelines are available here:
http://www.cps.gov.uk/legal/a_to_c/communications_sent_via_social_media/

EXPOSING ABUSERS

Abuse victims can apply to the High Court for an order to force a webmaster to provide details of posters' ISP addresses or names. However, social media websites like Facebook and Twitter are based in the US and are not subject to UK / EU laws.

During the first six months of 2013, Facebook received 1,975 requests from the UK, affecting 2,337 users (BBC News, 2013, *Government requests to Facebook outlined in report*).

Other figures show that Twitter responded to 158 requests during 2015 out of 442 in total (Twitter, 2015, *Transparency Report*).

In November 2016, Twitter unveiled new tools that users can use to deal with abusive messages. Its "mute" button is being extended to prevent Tweets containing chosen key words or phrases appearing in the notifications bar.

Users can also opt out of seeing conversations that include these key words. The mute button also enables users to not see Tweets from chosen individual accounts. There are also additional categories of offensive material.

People who wish to object to a Tweet can do so here: https://support.twitter.com/articles/20169998

They can also contact Lumen at https://lumendatabase.org/which will evaluate the complaint according to US law and publish it on its website.

Journalists who experience abuse should store copies of any relevant offensive material, including screenshots, for use in any subsequent court proceedings.

Case study

The High Court awarded a building industry expert £70,000 in libel damages over a cyberbullying campaign against him on Twitter and in a series of blogs. Richard Johnson was awarded the damages by Sir David Eady for repeated claims against him between November 2011 and June 2013.

The posts were read by possibly tens of thousands of people and included 129 Tweets over a 24-hour period. Eady described the abuse, which included allegations of misconduct, criminal offences and dishonesty, as "the most serious and distressing kind" (BAILLI, EWHC B24, 2014).

Case study

In November 2014, UK Independence Party (Ukip) MEP Jane Collins apologised (and made a donation to charity) after calling the head of a Christian charity a paedophile on Twitter during a by-election campaign. Her Tweet to Mark Russell, chief executive of the Church Army, included the words: "Yes, because we'd soon stop your criminal activity. Paedos leave our kids alone. #Ukip" (The Guardian, 2014, *Ukip MEP*). The Tweet was Retweeted repeatedly by Ukip supporters.

LAWS THAT CAN BE USED AGAINST ABUSERS

Trolling, cyberbullying and abuse fall into the following categories as far as the law is concerned.

Death threats

Perpetrators may be prosecuted under the Offences Against the Person Act 1861.

Stalking

Communications that target specific individuals may be treated as stalking under the Protection from Harassment Act (PHA) 1997. There have been no prosecutions to date because cyberbullies and abusers hide behind anonymity, and prosecutions must be brought against named individuals.

Harassment

Under the PHA, someone who sends two or more messages to the same person can be prosecuted and served with an injunction if they cause that person alarm or distress.

Malicious falsehood

A person can be sued if they publish false statements that are intended to damage a person or their business, commercial interests, goods or services.

Gross offence, indecency, obscenity or menace

The Communications Act (CA) 2003 applies to posts that are grossly offensive and could cause fear or apprehension.

Ministry of Justice statistics show that during 2014, 1,501 people (including 70 juveniles) were prosecuted for crimes under section 127 of the CA 2003, another 685 were cautioned, and 55 were jailed.

Fraud

Anyone who impersonates someone using a false social media account can be prosecuted under the Fraud Act 2006 if the account gives a misleading or untrue impression and causes the person loss or damage.

Pranksters often misuse Twitter by impersonating celebrities, famous people, and businesses. Twitter provides an online complaints form for victims. Blatant misrepresentation may also lead to prosecution for identity theft.

Threatening behaviour

Messages may be illegal if they make someone believe that physical harm is imminent, or if they threaten someone with violence, or damage to their property.

Promoting terrorism

The Terrorism Act 2006 makes it an offence to publish statements that directly or indirectly encourage people to commit, prepare, or instigate acts of terrorism.

Case study

In December 2014, a woman was jailed for promoting terrorism on Facebook. Runa Khan of Maple Road West, Luton, was jailed for five years after posting an online picture of a suicide vest, and one of her children holding guns and swords. She admitted to previously inciting terrorism in Syria (BBC News, 2014, *Runa Khan*).

Revealing personal information

Personal information should not be published without the consent of the individual involved, unless it is in the public domain already, or there is demonstrable public interest.

Personal privacy is protected by the:

1. DPA 1998.

2. ECHR article 8 (privacy).

3. Ipso / Ofcom codes of practice.

These cover personal information such as:

1. Medical details.

2. Financial information.

3. Work records.

4. Family relationships.

5. Sexual conduct.

6. Emotional / mental state.

7. Written or digital correspondence.

8. Social media records such as information or photographs from private Facebook or social media accounts.

Some Facebook users believe that the channel's facial recognition technology has privacy implications under the EU Data Protection Directive. However, a European class action by about 85,000 users against Facebook, alleging numerous privacy complaints, was rejected on procedural grounds.

Facebook changed its T&Cs from 1 January 2015 to give users greater control over how their content is shared, by adjusting their privacy and application settings.

In November 2016, Facebook agreed to suspend their use of UK WhatsApp users' data for advertisements or product improvement purposes.

This followed an investigation by the Information Commissioner, Elizabeth Denham, who was concerned that consumers were not being given adequate protection.

She said: "I don't think users have been given enough information about what Facebook plans to do with their information, and I don't think WhatsApp has got valid consent from users to share the information. I also believe users should be given ongoing control over how their information is used, not just a 30 day window" (ICO News Blog, 2016, *Information Commissioner updates on WhatsApp / Facebook investigation*).

The ICO has now asked Facebook and WhatsApp to sign an undertaking committed to better explaining to customers how their data will be used, and to giving users ongoing control over that information.

At the time of publication, Facebook and WhatsApp had not agreed and could face enforcement action if they use the data without valid consent

Ms Denham added: "It's a particular concern when company mergers mean that vast amounts of customers' personal data become an asset to be bought and sold."

Photographs usually represent a more significant invasion of privacy than words. Under-16s have greater privacy rights. This was established in the case of Weller and Others v. Associated Newspapers Limited, as noted below.

Case study

In 2012, the Mail Online published unpixelated photographs of singer Paul Weller's three children aged 10 months to 16 years. The singer sued for a breach of privacy and won £10,000 damages, despite the Mail Online arguing that the photographs were innocuous and taken in a public place (Courts and Tribunals Judiciary, 2012, *Weller -v- Associated Newspapers Ltd*).

In March 2016, the Supreme Court refused Associated Newspapers permission to appeal against the ruling. The Court of Appeal confirmed that although children do not have separate privacy rights, they may have a reasonable expectation of privacy on occasions where an adult does not.

Publishers should take into account factors such as:

1. The child's attributes.

2. What they are doing, and where.

3. The nature and purpose of the intrusion.

4. Whether consent was given.

5. The effect on the child.

The ruling effectively prevents the media from publishing images of children without consent.

Case study

In 2012, the Sun newspaper published photographs taken from Facebook which showed Kate Winslet's new husband Ned RocknRoll semi-naked at a fancy dress party.

Mr Justice Briggs banned the newspaper from reusing the photographs because they could have led to Ms Winslet's children being ridiculed. The Sun argued that RocknRoll became a public figure when he married Winslet and that he had waived his rights to privacy after he was paid for publicity about his first marriage, in 2009. It also said that the photographs were visible to anyone with a Facebook account (Pinsent Masons Out-Law.com, 2013, *Privacy rights existed despite RocknRoll Facebook photos being accessible by public, rules High Court*).

Case study

In March 2016, the Court of Appeal issued an interim injunction preventing the Sun on Sunday from revealing the identity of a married celebrity who had been involved in a sexual threesome.

The injunction will remain in place until a full hearing, and means that no UK media can name the man, even though he is being named in other countries, and on social media.

The court ruled that the celebrity's right to private and family life overrode the newspaper's right to publish details about the extramarital sexual activities. The celebrity is married to someone also involved in the entertainments industry.

Lord Justice Jackson said the court was acting out of concern for the welfare of the children of the married couple. He said it was necessary to consider the children, because "even if the children do not suffer harassment in the short-term, they are bound to learn about these matters from school friends and the internet in due course" (BAILII, EWCA Civ 100, 2016).

HATE CRIMES

In the online environment, the criminal offences mentioned above can also be defined as hate crimes if they constitute hostility or prejudice based on:

1. Disability.
2. Race.
3. Religion.
4. Transgender identity.
5. Sexual orientation.

If there is evidence of a hate crime when someone is convicted for another offence, the judge can impose a tougher sentence under the Criminal Justice Act 2003.

Hate crimes law has raised concerns from some journalists about freedom of speech. "Hatred" is subjective, and some critics have attached the "hate" label to comments that are simply robust debates, criticism or satire.

SEXTING

The Criminal Justice and Courts Act 2015 makes sexting, or "revenge porn", a crime. Anyone who sends or receives a sexually explicit text, image or video footage on a mobile phone or tablet, or posts them online, with intent to cause distress, can be charged.

This law may cause an ethical dilemma for editors, as it does not provide complainants with anonymity. This lack of protection from publicity may deter victims from making a complaint to the police, and media coverage could draw further attention to the offensive images, and make a complaint counter-productive.

However, on the other side of the coin, if complainants are given anonymity, then it is likely that the identities of their alleged abusers may also be protected, as naming them would reveal the names of the complainant.

As things stand, the only options for complainants is to either apply for witness anonymity under the Coroners and Justice Act 2009, or to ask their solicitor to apply for a section 11 order under the CCA 1981, if the allegation resulted in a court case. However, web editors must be prepared for victims to ask them to provide anonymity voluntarily. There is certainly an ethical argument for doing so.

Journalists investigating allegations of sexting should discourage alleged victims from sending them the images involved because they may inadvertently commit an offence under the Protection of Children Act 1978 by storing indecent images of a person under 18 on a smartphone or other device.

SEXTORTION

In November 2016, the National Crime Agency (NCA) reported that four British men had committed suicide in the previous year in cases linked to "sextortion".

The NCA also said that the number of people reporting webcam blackmails has more than doubled from 385 in 2015 to 864 up to November 2016 (NCA, 2016, *Help available for webcam blackmail victims: don't panic, and don't pay*).

"Sextortion" is a form of blackmail where criminals use fake identities to befriend victims online before persuading them to perform sexual acts in front of their webcams.

SECURITY AND PRIVACY

PROTECTING SOURCES

In April 2013, former Guardian newspaper editor Alan Rusbridger made an important speech reminding everybody that journalists had a duty to protect their sources.

The Ipso and Ofcom codes require journalists to protect confidential sources of information. In addition, the CCA says they should only reveal sources if a High Court judge passes an order for them to do so in the interests of justice or national security, or for the prevention of disorder or crime. A judge must consider freedom of expression under the ECHR when considering passing an order.

Journalists should reveal the source of a story only to their editor or line manager, and should take professional and legal advice if a police officer or government official asks them to reveal a source.

Case study

In August 2015, the Big Issue North published an interview with the victim of a Rotherham sex abuse gang, which had been commissioned from a freelance journalist (Big Issue North, 2015, *They don't scare me now*).

A few months later, an NCA investigator emailed the editor, Kevin Gopal, asking for a meeting so that the police could recover anything that Big Issue North had relating to the published article or otherwise, to assist them with the investigation.

Mr Gopal declined. He told the investigator that he had a duty to protect his sources, and was not legally obliged to

> hand over journalistic material. He also advised the freelance journalist to secure the material, in case the police tried to use Ripa (Regulation of Investigatory Powers Act) to obtain it.
>
> So far, the police have not made another request for the information.

In practice, social media and Instant Messages (IM) make it difficult for journalists to keep their contacts secure. To avoid unintentionally exposing sources, journalists should:

1. Provide a drop box for sensitive documents.

2. Tell sources not to communicate with them via public social media pages.

3. Check to whom they are connected on LinkedIn and similar websites. Their contacts might not want other people to know that they are connected to a journalist.

4. Beware of Tweeting that they are meeting someone, and remember to turn off location services when meeting contacts privately.

5. Use separate social media accounts for work, and choose "friends" carefully.

6. Use messaging apps like WhatsApp that provide encryption.

RISKS POSED BY THE "GRIM RIPA" AND ITS SUCCESSOR

The Regulation of Investigatory Powers Act (Ripa) 2000 has now been replaced by the Investigatory Powers Act 2016 (IPA).

Ripa proved to be one of the most controversial pieces of legislation to have affected journalists, and the IPA is expected to present an even graver threat.

Ripa gave the police and some other public authorities the power to apply to the home secretary for an order that allowed them to access a journalist's email messages, telephone records and other digital data.

For example, police investigating the former MP Chris Huhne's speeding fraud secretly obtained a Mail on Sunday reporter's telephone records without his consent (The Guardian, 2014, *Police secretly obtained reporter's phone records in Huhne investigation*).

In another incident, police investigating the Plebgate saga obtained the telephone records of the Sun newspaper's political editor, Tom Newton Dunn (The Guardian, 2014, *Plebgate*).

These examples were the tip of the iceberg. Figures show that the police made more than 6,000 Ripa applications in 2013, compared with just over 60 in 2002. In February 2015, a report by the Interception of Communications Commissioner's Office revealed that 19 police forces had used Ripa 608 times to uncover journalistic data over three years.

The IPA became law in December 2016. It requires web and phone companies to store records of websites visited by every citizen (including journalists) for 12 months, for access by police, security services and other public bodies. It allows security services to acquire bulk collections of communications data, such as mobile phone records.

The act gives special protection to journalists' data and sources, but many critics fear these do not go far enough, and have labelled it the "Snoopers' Charter".

A letter to The Guardian newspaper in March 2016, signed by more than 200 lawyers, claimed that the bill was not fit for purpose and breached international standards on surveillance (The Guardian, 2016, *Investigatory powers bill not up to the task*).

SAFE DIGITAL PRACTICE

Unfortunately, many editorial computer systems do not allow reporters to browse anonymously nor do they offer basic encryption, and the webmasters can easily read email messages sent to and from journalists' work email accounts.

When working on sensitive stories, journalists should:

1. Use a private, encrypted browser like Tor.

2. Use a personal, encrypted webmail account for sensitive stories.

3. Encrypt IMs and scramble social media conversations when possible.

4. Secure their home Wi-Fi network.

5. Use complex passwords on all web accounts.

6. Make telephone calls using a pay-as-you-go mobile phone, paid for in cash or with an Amazon voucher.

7. Record contact details in a paper book, and store it at home.

8. Avoid promising someone anonymity unless they are certain they can achieve it.

Journalists should remember that if contacts are stored on an employer's computer, those contacts belong to the employer, and journalists could be in breach of the DPA if they download the contacts when leaving the company.

The same applies to their contacts on LinkedIn and similar platforms. If journalists use their employer's computer facilities and their business email address to create a LinkedIn account, courts are likely to consider that the content belongs to the employer.

COMPUTER MISUSE

Journalists have a legal and ethical duty to respect other people's digital privacy. The infamous phone hacking trial has shown beyond doubt that it is a criminal offence under the Computer Misuse Act (CMA) to hack someone's telephone, mobile phone, tablet or computer, or to alter, transfer or copy files without permission.

An addition, clause 10 of the Editors' Code of Practice states:

> "The press must not seek to obtain or publish material acquired by using hidden cameras or clandestine listening devices; or by intercepting private or mobile telephone calls, messages or emails; or by the unauthorised removal of documents or photographs; or by accessing digitally-held private information without consent" (Ipso, 2015, *Editors' Code of Practice*).

This clause can be breached in the public interest, but no such defence exists under the CMA.

DATA PROTECTION

Media organisations have a duty under the DPA to store people's names, addresses and other personal information securely, and to process it fairly and lawfully.

The act gives people the right to ask media organisations for a copy of information held about them, using a "subject access request". However, editors can reject these requests and avoid most other requirements under the DPA by using the journalistic exemption provided under section 32. If they do so, the person who requested the information can complain to the ICO, Ipso or Ofcom.

Although such complaints are unlikely to succeed, media organisations must nonetheless have procedures for handling subject access requests, especially as the "right to be forgotten" ruling, mentioned earlier, may trigger more requests.

The ICO published new DPA media guidelines in September 2015. Publication was originally delayed because some media organisations complained that they represented a chilling effect on journalism, threatened investigations, and did not reflect the day-to-day reality of journalism.

JOURNALISTS AND DATA PROTECTION OFFENCES

The DPA makes it a criminal offence for a journalist to knowingly or recklessly obtain personal data from another organisation without its consent; for example, by subterfuge, misrepresentation or hacking. The offence provides a public interest defence, but a stricter threshold is applied.

USE OF DRONES

Many UK media organisations use drones to shoot video footage in difficult locations, or for investigative assignments. Journalists are entitled to use drones for surveillance provided they are necessary and the story is in the public interest under the Ipso and Ofcom regulatory codes. These activities are also covered by the DPA, although the journalistic exemption applies.

However, the ICO has advised the media to be open and honest with the public when they are using drones, as their use can arouse concern. Some media organisations use signs to tell the public when they are filming.

If someone complains about covert filming, the ICO will weigh up the:

1. Importance of the story.

2. Level of intrusion.

3. Potential impact upon the individual and any third parties.

The ICO's guidelines for surveillance cameras can be downloaded as a PDF here: https://ico.org.uk/media/for-organisations/documents/1542/cctv-code-of-practice.pdf

A list of other laws that affect users of drones can be seen here: http://www.caa.co.uk/Commercial-Industry/Aircraft/Unmanned-aircraft/Unmanned-Aircraft/

LAWS THAT JOURNALISTS CAN USE

There are some laws that can help journalists gather information.

FREEDOM OF INFORMATION ACT (FOIA)

This law gives journalists the right to access information held by more than 100,000 publicly funded bodies, ranging from hospitals and schools to quangos and government departments. Since its inception in 2005, it has provided journalists with information for countless stories that would have not been reported, otherwise. These include the infamous MPs' expenses scandal of 2009, and the report in July 2015 that UK pilots had taken part in coalition air strikes over Syria.

Revelations like these may explain why former Prime Minister Tony Blair, in his memoirs, called himself a "foolish, irresponsible nincompoop" (Blair, 2011, *A Journey*, p.516), for introducing the act. The act allows anyone, press and public, to make written requests for information from any public body. The body must respond within 20 working days and may not ask why the information is being requested. If the body concerned refuses a request, it must usually provide a reason, and it can reject vexatious requests or those that are disproportionately expensive (ICO, n.d., *When can we refuse a request for information?*)

If information appears to have been wrongly withheld, the person who asked for it can complain to the ICO.

There was some concern among journalists in 2015 when the government announced a review of the FOIA. Many feared the Independent Commission on Freedom of Information would limit the act's scope.

However, the review's report said there was no evidence that the FOIA needed substantial amendments. The government accepted its recommendations in February 2016, and said the act did not require any "legal changes". Nevertheless, this does not stop it implementing smaller changes recommended by the review, by altering ICO guidelines.

One area it may consider is the timeframe a public authority may be allocated when considering whether a request has a public interest dimension. Currently, the deadline can be extended by an unspecified period. However, the report recommends limiting this to a further 20 working days.

Exempt categories

The act lists 23 types of exemptions that bodies can use to avoid disclosing information. The exemptions can be seen here:

http://www.lboro.ac.uk/admin/ar/policy/foi/exemptions/

If a journalist believes an information request has been turned down for the wrong reasons, they should initially complain to the body involved, and ask them to review the decision.

If this does not produce a satisfactory outcome, they can complain to the ICO, which will try to resolve the issues informally.

If the journalist is still dissatisfied with the outcome, they can take the matter further, using the ICO's complaints process, which can be found on this downloadable PDF:

https://ico.org.uk/media/for-organisations/documents/1215/complaints_guide_for_public_authorities.pdf

Case study

In 2015, Tom Wall, an environmental journalist and digital editor of the Environmental Health News achieved a victory over the ICO over his attempt to obtain information about bad landlords, under the FOIA. Environmental Health News is the official magazine for the Chartered Institute of Environmental Health.

A tribunal ordered the Ministry of Justice (MoJ) to hand over the information on convicted landlords to Wall, after it rejected the ICO's decision that the information should be kept secret.

Wall wanted details of landlords convicted of environmental health offences under the Housing Act 2004 so that local authorities could be warned about using them in the future. The landlords had been convicted for failing to meet government standards of accommodation, such as warmth and provision of basic facilities.

It took Wall more than a year to win his case after his Freedom of Information request was rejected by the MoJ and then the ICO.

The ICO said the information was "sensitive personal data" and rejected Wall's public interest argument. However, the First-Tier (Information Rights) Tribunal unanimously ruled in Wall's favour (Information Tribunal, 2015, *Appeal No: EA/2014/0265*).

Wall told Online Law for Journalists: "It is troubling that is took me so long to obtain this information. It should have been freely available to the press.

"Many journalists would have been forced to give up long ago. I'm lucky I have generous and supportive colleagues who allowed me to pursue this story to the very end. But

> how many other good leads have been abandoned by hard-pressed reporters and campaigners without the time to challenge Britain's culture of unthinking official secrecy?"

Wall's observations confirm what many journalists feared when the FOIA was introduced. It is a law that cuts both ways. It gives them access to some information, but it also enables authorities to withhold other material or make it too difficult and expensive to access it.

How to submit a request

Requests under the FOIA must be made to the authority's information officer, or equivalent. However, many journalists use the excellent website https://www.whatdotheyknow.com/ for FOIA requests (What do they know, n.d., *Browse And Search Requests*). This website has archived almost 300,000 FOIA responses from more than 16,000 public bodies. New requests can be submitted using an online form.

ENVIRONMENTAL INFORMATION REGULATIONS (EIR) 2004

The EIR are similar to the FOIA but apply to information relating to the environment. A journalist researching anything from GM crops to flooding, and climate change to swine flu can ask public authorities to provide them with information. EIR requests can be made verbally.

However, like the FOIA, the EIR has exemptions that allow the body to reject information requests by sending the requester a refusal notice.

The exemptions include unfinished documents, internal communications, requests that are "manifestly unreasonable" or those where disclosure would be harmful.

The EIR is administered by the ICO, which has a separate complaints procedure that journalists can use. See details:

https://ico.org.uk/for-organisations/guide-to-the-environmental-information-regulations/complaints/

DATA PROTECTION ACT (DPA) 1998

Journalists tend to see the DPA as "an enemy" but, in fact, they can use it to research stories by asking a contact to access their personal information from an authority, and pass it to the journalist to use in a story. For instance, a journalist doing a story about a mistake made in a hospital operation could get quotes and general information about the operation, using the FOIA if necessary. And, they could also ask the person they are writing about to ask the hospital for their personal medical files, under the DPA.

Although the DPA invariably trumps FOIA requests that involve personal information, journalists can argue that information should be released in the public interest if it concerns an official's public role. For instance, a journalist may be investigating a story about the chair of a quango who has allegedly used his influence to give a top job to an unqualified friend. The friend's details would normally be protected by the DPA. However, the journalist might be able to access her CV under the FOIA, arguing that her private information has a significant impact on her public role.

Case studies

Two rulings by the Information Tribunal (IT) in early 2016 demonstrate the balancing act that authorities must perform when considering FOIA requests that involve people's personal details.

The IT ruled that Swansea Council was not required to release details of an internal investigation into why a council officer was not fined for parking on double yellow lines in the presence of traffic wardens.

It said it would be disproportionate and unfair to disclose the details of the investigation, as to do so would be unusual and it could be professionally detrimental to those involved; the officer, who had middle management status, had a reasonable expectation of confidentiality.

It was relevant that the case had already attracted publicity because a video of the car parking incident was posted online (Information Tribunal, 2016, *Steve Pritchard and Information Commissioner EA/2015/0175*).

In contrast, Bolton Council was ordered to name a councillor who failed to pay council tax, saying that the councillor would not be disproportionately prejudiced if the information was released. It also said the public had a right know whether elected officials were fulfilling their duties, especially as failure to pay council tax can result in a councillor being disqualified from voting on a council's budget (BAILII, UKUT 139 (AAC) 2016).

COPYRIGHT

Journalists often want to use other people's content and, therefore, should have a good knowledge of copyright laws. Copyright is more strictly enforced on the internet than it used to be, and journalists can expect to receive an invoice should they use someone else's content without consent.

This is especially the case with images. In July 2016, The Guardian newspaper reported that a leading regional newspaper publisher had warned editorial staff about using images without proper consent.

The Guardian's report also stated that Newsquest's head of legal, Simon Westrop, told staff not to publish a picture obtained from Google or any other online source without checking that they either had the legal right to use it, or a sound legal defence (The Guardian, 2016, *Newsquest hit by growing copyright claims over use of photographs*).

Copyright law is simple: if someone does not own the copyright, someone else does. And, if a journalist wishes to use third-party content, they must usually get consent, credit the copyright owners, and possibly pay for the use.

Copyright is covered by the Copyright Designs and Patents Act (CDPA) 1998 (UK Legislation, n.d., *Copyright, Designs and Patents Act*), which has been amended by several EU directives. The EU plans eventually to have a single EU copyright code and copyright title, and a single copyright jurisdiction and tribunal. It remains to be seen whether the UK signs up to this code after Brexit.

Similar pan-European rights for trademarks and patents already exist, so the plan is not as far-fetched as it sounds, although the 2016 deadline appears optimistic.

Copyright law protects the products of people's skill, labour, creativity and time and is usually owned by the person who created a work, unless it was commissioned by someone else. It usually lasts for 70 years after the originator's death, no matter who owns the copyright.

WHAT COPYRIGHT LAW COVERS

Work must be "fixed" in order for copyright to apply, that is: written down, recorded, filmed, inputted onto a PC, photographed etc.

Copyright automatically applies to the following:

1. Written content.

2. Music.

3. Photographs, logos and graphics, even if they are modified to create a "new" image.

4. Audio recordings.

5. Films, TV programmes and videos.

6. Magazine or newspaper design: the fonts, colours, layout.

7. Databases.

WHAT COPYRIGHT LAW DOES NOT COVER

There is no copyright on news, facts, ideas or information. Copyright only applies to the way these are selected, arranged, and presented to create an original work. However, persistent lifting of facts from another publication, even if they are rewritten each time, may be seen as an infringement.

WHO OWNS COPYRIGHT

Copyright applies automatically; it does not have to be registered. However, there are varying arrangements for certain situations.

Freelance writers and photographers own the copyright to their work unless they have signed an agreement to the contrary. Many newspapers and magazines commission work on the basis that the copyright belongs to them, and this can be very unpopular with freelancers who stand to lose money by signing away their syndications rights.

Case study

A ruling in 2015 by the Court of Justice of the European Union (CJEU) allows photographers to sue for copyright breaches in the UK courts if their photographs have been used in another EU country. In the past, actions had to be brought in the country where the photographs were published.

An Austrian photographer, Ms Pez Hejduk, brought a copyright claim in an Austrian court, claiming that a German company EnergieAgentur had used her photographs on their website without consent. The company said she should have brought the action in Germany, as their website was not aimed at the Austrian market.

However, the CJEU said that damage had occurred in Austria because Ms Hejduk's photographs were accessible online there, and that her copyright was protected by Austrian law. The ruling may help UK photographers and publishers whose images are published on websites in other

> EU countries (Info Curia Case-law of the Court of Justice, 2015, *Pez Hejduk v. EnergieAgentur*).

People own the copyright to their letters published on newspaper and magazine letters' pages, but they license the publisher for one free use.

Copyright can apply to the spoken word but speakers must assert their rights in writing, in advance. Speakers can also restrict who uses their words. So, someone may give a freelance journalist an interview on the condition that the journalist can only sell it to the Daily Telegraph or the Daily Express. However, these restrictions do not apply when people are speaking in the course of their employment or in speeches made in parliamentary or judicial proceedings.

Incidental breaches of copyright are allowed. For instance, if a photographer takes a photograph of a man for a feature about his charity work, and it happens to include a copyright painting in the shot, his photographs will not breach the painter's copyright.

IMAGES TAKEN ON MOBILE PHONES

Many journalists and members of the public assume that copyright always applies to photographs taken on smartphones.

In fact, the situation is less clear-cut following a judgment by the ECJ in the case Eva-Maria Painer v Standard VerlagsGmbH and others in 2011.

The judges said that items like photographs could be copyright if they were "original" in the sense that they are intellectual creations and that they show an element of creative skill. In other words, that they reflect the author's personality, and that the author expressed their creative abilities by making free and creative choices when they took them (BAILII, C14510, 2011). So, it could be argued that photographs that are taken on smartphones on the spur of the moment do not provide the author the opportunity to express their creative abilities, so are therefore not automatically copyright.

Also, the owner of a "selfie" or similar "snatch" photograph may have difficulty arguing that the image involved the use of "skill, labour and time".

FAIR DEALING

Fair dealing is a valuable tool for journalists. It is sometimes called fair use (mainly in the US), and allows free use of substantial extracts of copyright work in certain circumstances, provided the copyright owner is given a suitable credit.

"Substantial" is usually taken to mean up to one third of the original content, but may also depend on the proportion the extract makes up in the article. The courts will also look at the extract's commercial value. So, if a small excerpt is taken from a short but highly specialised publication, this might be construed as infringement. Courts over the years have made it clear that "substantial" can refer to quality, or quantity.

What fair dealing covers:

1. **Reports of current events**. Photographs are not included. It allows publishers to use extracts of copyright work in order to report events contemporaneously, and to report past events that are still genuinely newsworthy.

2. **Private study or research for a non-commercial purpose**. However, research for an article to be

published in a newspaper or a magazine is regarded as a commercial purpose, so fair dealing does not apply.

3. **Criticism or review**. This includes extracts and photographs from books, plays, films, and broadcasts to be included in a review. A journalist should quote only as much material as they need to make their point.

4. **Quotations**. This allows extracts from copyright works to be used to provide a "quote" in the traditional sense of the word, but also to reference something that has already happened. For example, clips from various movies could be shown to illustrate the fact that a particular actor favours comedy roles.

5. **Caricature, parody or pastiche**. This allows publishers to take an extract from a copyright work and build on it to create a separate "mashed-up" work, usually for humorous effect. The IPO explains in its guidance, "Exceptions to Copyright – Guidance for Creators and Copyright Owners": "a comedian may use a few lines from a film or song for a parody sketch; a cartoonist may reference a well-known artwork or illustration for a caricature; an artist may use small fragments from a range of films to compose a larger pastiche artwork" (GOV.UK, 2014, *Changes to Copyright Law*).

Case study

There has also been some uncertainty as to whether copyright applies to brief video clips used on apps like Vine, Periscope, and animated gifs.

In March 2016, the High Court gave a partial answer in the case England and Wales Cricket Board and Sky UK Limited vs Tixdaq Limited and Fanatix Limited.

The case involved Fanatix's iOS app, which allowed users to upload, share and comment on short clips of sports footage.

Sky argued that these clips infringed their copyright, while the defendants said they counted as fair dealing (the reporting of current events).

Mr Justice Arnold had to decide whether eight-second clips constituted a "substantial" part of the original broadcast which lasted up to two hours; and, if they did, whether they counted as fair dealing.

The judge ruled that the short clips were substantial, not in terms of quantity, but quality, as they showed the important highlights. He also decided that they did not constitute fair dealing.

He said: "The clips were not used in order to inform the audience about a current event, but presented for consumption because of their intrinsic interest and value. Furthermore, although the fact that a news service is a commercial one funded by advertising revenue does not prevent its use from being for the purpose of reporting current events, I consider that the defendants' objective was purely commercial rather than genuinely informatory" (BAILII, EWHC 575, 2016).

MORAL RIGHTS

Anyone who commissions a photograph from a freelancer or studio for private or domestic use has the right to veto publication, even if they do not own the copyright.

This means that journalists who "borrow" photographs or download them from social media platforms like Facebook should obtain copyright consent from the people who took the photographs, as well as permission to publish them from the people who commissioned them.

Copyright law also provides three other moral rights:

1. The right to be identified as the copyright owner.

2. The right not to have the work subject to derogatory treatment.

    This is defined as any addition, deletion, alteration to or adaptation of a work that amounts to a distortion or mutilation of the work, or is otherwise prejudicial to the honour or reputation of the author. However, this does not apply to work produced for the news media – presumably to prevent contributors objecting to it being subjected to the mercy of sub editors.

3. The right to object to false attribution. This prevents instances where, for example, a journalist interviewed someone, and then used their quotes with a byline, implying that the speaker actually wrote the article.

COPYRIGHT BREACHES

Most copyright disputes involving journalists are dealt with by the Intellectual Property Enterprise Court small claims track, which handles claims of up to £10,000.

The onus is on the copyright owner to prove that the work is original.

The copyright owner can:

1. Obtain an injunction preventing further infringement.

2.　Obtain damages and costs.

3.　Obtain an order for the possession of the copyright work and any equipment used in the infringement.

4.　Force the defendant to account for the profits made from the infringement.

Copyright licensing disputes are handled by the Copyright Tribunal.

COPYRIGHT DEFENCES

The main copyright defences are:

1. **Public interest**. This defence is unclear, but may apply if there is a strong public interest in the copyright material.

2. **Innocent infringement.** This applies if the infringer did not know and had no reason to believe that the work was copyright; for example, they believed it had expired.

3. **Consent**. This can either be express consent, such as contract or agreement; or implied consent judged according to the circumstances, correspondence etc.

ONLINE CONTENT

Journalists own their online content including photographs, videos, Tweets, status updates on Facebook, LinkedIn and other social media websites, blogs, and comments they make on other peoples' websites.

However, when they sign up to social media channels such as Facebook, Flickr, Twitter, Instagram and YouTube, they give these websites the right to adapt, distribute and use their content in promotional material, worldwide. With Twitter this includes live streams using an app like Periscope.

In March 2016, Ed Vaizey, as minister for culture, media and sport, reminded social media users that taking and sharing screenshots of Snapchat images was a breach of copyright.

In an answer to a written question, he said: "Under UK copyright law, it would be unlawful for a Snapchat user to copy an image and make it available to the public without the consent of the image owner. The image owner would be able to sue anyone who does this for copyright infringement" (They Work for You, 2016, *Social Networking: Photographs*).

It is unclear why Mr Vaizey singled out Snapchat for special treatment, because copyright law covers all other similar social media channels. It also needs to be clarified that it may be arguable whether the content of a screenshot was the product of the originator's "skill, labour and time", as required by the CDPA.

People who share screenshots via Snapchat, Twitter and other platforms may be able defend themselves under the rules of fair dealing, or claim the copyright owner – who may not be the sender – gave implied copyright consent.

Snapchat photographs are automatically deleted after 10 seconds. The Snapchat privacy policy states that if Snapchat detects that a recipient has taken a screenshot of an image, they will try to inform the original poster. However, Snapchat advises users to avoid sending messages that they would not want someone to save or share.

Mr Vaizey also warned that sharing private sexual photographs or films can breach the Criminal Justice and Courts Act 2015. For more information on this, see the section on Sexting under the heading Online Abuse.

Web editors may face take-down requests under the Digital Economy Act 2010, if an online visitor posts a photograph belonging to someone else on a message board. If a web editor receives a request, they should:

1. Check that is it valid.

2. Remove the photograph.

3. Give the contributor a written warning.

4. Tell them where they can get the image legally.

5. Record the details, as the copyright owner can also get a court order requiring the website to reveal the IP address owner's details.

A new digital economy bill, which is due to come into force this year (2017) increases criminal penalties for online copyright infringement to include imprisonment for up to 10 years. Currently it stands at two years (UK Parliament, n.d., *Digital Economy Bill (HL Bill 80)*).

CREATIVE COMMONS LICENSE (CCL)

Some copyright owners allow other users to use their work under any one of six CCLs, which can be viewed here: http://creativecommons.org/licenses/

This is a valuable facility for journalists and bloggers. However, they should check the licence conditions before publishing any material, and adhere to the T&Cs.

COPYRIGHT OF TWEETS

Tweets are unlikely to be long enough to receive protection under the CDPA, although this issue has not yet been dealt with by UK courts. However, the ECJ decided, in the case of

Infopaq International A/S v Danske Dagblades Forening, in 2011, that as few as 11 words qualify for protection provided they are the "expression of the intellectual creation of its author" (European Commission, 2009, *Infopaq International A/S v Danske Dagblades Forening, judgment of 16 July 2009*).

This means that copyright could apply if someone Tweets or Retweets:

1. A short poem, like a haiku.

2. An original saying or proverb.

3. A poem, one line at a time.

The ECJ has left it to national courts to decide their stance in each case.

In 2012, Twitter changed its procedures for copyright complaints made under the US Digital Millennium Copyright Act 1998. Twitter now "withholds" the Tweets, and posts its own Tweet explaining why the "offensive" Tweet no longer appears. It used to simply remove them, leaving people wondering why they had been taken down.

COPYRIGHT AND PINTEREST

Journalists face two contrasting issues with the virtual pinboard site, Pinterest.

First, they should get consent before publishing other people's images. Second, they should monitor the site for illegal uses of their own images.

Pinterest has different T&Cs from Facebook and similar sites. Account holders are responsible for checking the copyright of everything they post, as well as for the full cost of any legal action that could follow. This includes actions against

Pinterest's owners, Cold Brew Labs. In reality, however, few users check copyright before they pin.

The website differs from Google image results, because Google does not actually store copies of the images it displays, whereas Pinterest does. It is also different to social media sites, which just display a thumbnail of the image, with a link back to the source.

Pinterest stores a full-size copy of each image, and allows visitors to re-pin images on their own pages, thus facilitating further copyright breaches. However, it does not take responsibility for copyright breaches. Its T&Cs place the liability with the person who made the pin. However, Pinterest will remove copyright images on request.

Some journalists and media groups are happy to allow extracts from their publications to be "pinned". Others opt to use a special code on their images that prevents them being copied to Pinterest.

TRADEMARKS

THE LAW

Trademarks were protected under the Trademark Act 1994 until March 2016.

However, the act has been superseded by the EU Trademarks Directive, which will harmonise trademark law across the EU. Member states have until January 2019 to incorporate the directive into their national laws.

It is unlikely the directive will result in significant changes for journalists.

TRADEMARKS ARE IMPORTANT

Most companies guard trademarks ferociously. They are valuable commodities, and businesses spend millions to distinguish them from their rivals. They will not tolerate any breaches.

Once a trademark starts to be used as a noun or verb, there is a real risk that its distinctiveness will be eroded, diluted or even lost entirely. And, when that happens, the trademark may be revoked because it has become genericised.

This means a trademark becomes synonymous with all products of its kind. For example, people say they are "doing the hoovering", even if they are using a Dyson or a Vax. Businesses do not want their products lumped together with all the others.

Should journalists or bloggers use trademarks incorrectly, they can expect to receive letters of complaint from the businesses that own the trademarks, followed by court action if the mistakes are not rectified.

Because trademarks are valuable, businesses want to keep them distinctive, so journalists should:

1. Check for registration of trademarked words and images on the IPO website (GOV.UK, n.d., *Intellectual Property Office*).

2. Use trademarks correctly and use the ® symbol if the trademark is registered.

3. Use generic words instead of trademarked words, to avoid a complaint. For instance, it would be better to refer to "painkillers" rather than "Aspirin".

Check for trademark registration

The easiest way to check whether words are trademarks is to use the IPO website: http://www.ipo.gov.uk/types/tm/t-os/t-find.htm

This is not an exhaustive list.

Some trademarks are registered on a "word only" basis. This means that only the pure text is trademarked; others are trademarked as "stylised words" which are used as part of a logo, or written only in a specific typeface.

When referring to protected company or product names, the term to use is "trademark". The terms "copyright" or "patent-protected", are different and not related to trademark law.

How to use trademarks correctly

It is important to not only check whether a word is a trademark, but to also make sure that the item being referred to was made by that company, and not another. For example, if a portable cabin is not made by Portakabin, it must simply be called a portable cabin, and not a Portakabin.

Aspirin, sellotape and escalator are all trademarks, but have been absorbed into language as generic terms. So have portacabins and google. This does not mean that these generic terms can be used in copy. Therefore, a reference to someone "doing the hoovering" should be changed to someone "doing the vacuuming with a Hoover® vacuum cleaner".

It is also a good idea to check whether using the trademarked name is important in context. It might be sufficient to say "used a paper tissue" rather than to say "used a Kleenex® tissue", unless the trademark is important to the story.

How to write trademarks

Trademarks should:

1. Be spelled correctly eg Portakabin, not Portacabin.

2. Be capitalised appropriately eg Kleenex, not kleenex.

3. Be used as an adjective followed by the appropriate noun eg: "wiped with a Kleenex® tissue", not "wiped with a Kleenex®".

4. Be followed by the ® symbol if they are registered; not all trademarks are registered. TM means nothing in the UK.

5. Never be pluralised eg (Jiffies)

6. Never be used in the possessive form (Kleenex's tissues)

7. Never be used as verbs (I am going to google it.)

Some companies are not too bothered about affixing the ® symbol when they write their own trademarks, whereas others are very explicit about its use. For example, Kleenex® uses the ® symbol in certain contexts but not in others.

And, some publications and websites do not use the ® symbol after registered trademarks. However, should a journalist or blogger be in doubt, they should follow the law.

For more details on how to write trademarks, see:

http://www.ipo.gov.uk/types/tm/t-manage/t-enforce.htm

Archiving Digital Data and Images

Website operators should retain digital data in case they receive a complaint or need to use the data in a court case. Courts also have the power to request disclosure of deleted documents, and can impose penalties if anyone attempts to amend or delete documents that might be required as evidence.

Staff journalists should not use their own digital devices or social media accounts for work, because their editors or publishers might not be able to access the data, should it be required. Web editors should set clear rules about data retention for IM, email, web activity logs, text messages, and history from Facebook, Twitter and similar websites.

Online Archives

Below is listed the main risks related to online archives.

Defamation

Online publishers who republish defamatory items may be protected under the DA 2013. See the section called "What a libel claimant has to prove", under Defamation, above.

Case study

In February 2014, the High Court ruled that an archived news report could lose the protection of qualified privilege should circumstances change. The ruling, in the case Flood v Times Newspapers Ltd, means that publishers should consider updating or amending online content if someone who once faced an accusation has since been cleared (5RB, n.d., *Flood v Times Newspapers Limited*).

In addition, Ofcom or Ipso may order webmasters running UK magazine and newspaper websites to remove items that have breached the various codes of practice.

Restricted identities

An online archive may contain content or images of someone who subsequently receives legal anonymity. It is safe to retain the content, but attention should not be drawn to it, nor should articles include new links to it, either manually or automatically. "Similar stories" tools can cause problems here, and need to be monitored.

Web editors should respond quickly to legitimate take-down requests from courts, the police or the Attorney General.

Use of incorrect images

Using an incorrect photograph from an archive can be defamatory, especially if used to depict a criminal or someone involved in insalubrious activities.

Archived photographs should be tagged with clear identification details, especially if the photographs include images of people who have common names.

Case study

In November 2013, E! Online published a picture of Steps' singer Ian "H" Watkins instead of the Lostprophets' front man, Ian Watkins, when reporting a child abuse case.

Paedophile Ian Watkins, 36, of Pontypridd, lead singer of the now-disbanded rock group Lostprophets, admitted to a string of child sex abuse charges, including attempted rape of a baby, at Cardiff Crown Court.

In a statement, an E! Online spokeswoman said: "E! Online deeply regrets originally publishing an image of Ian "H" Watkins of the band Steps, rather than Ian Watkins of Lostprophets, and the error was corrected immediately" (The Telegraph, 2013, *Steps star H wins public apology after being wrongly pictured as paedophile*).

Stock images

Reusing archived photographs may breach an individual's right to privacy. A web editor or blogger may need fresh consent to use a photograph in a story with a different context.

For example, a news website might publish (with consent) a photograph of a man smoking outside a hospital's accident and emergency department while waiting to see if his wife had survived a serious car accident.

But, it would probably be a breach of the man's privacy rights if the website later used the same image to accompany a feature on the effects of a smoking ban imposed in the hospital grounds.

Just because someone consents to being photographed in one situation does not mean they have given their consent to disimilar re-uses.

Other dangers

Other dangers include:

1. Republishing an article about a defendant's conviction may be defamatory if they have since been cleared on appeal.

2. Republishing old court copy means that the libel protection drops from absolute privilege to qualified privilege, which stipulates that copy should not be published with malice.

3. Republishing details of someone's previous crimes and convictions could breach the Rehabilitation of Offenders Act 1974. Again, publishing with malice could create a problem defending a libel claim.

4. As mentioned above, a website's automatic "similar stories" function might display someone's previous convictions or other information which could prejudice their trial.

5. An article or photograph may refer to changed circumstances. For instance, a story about a husband and wife who are happily married could be defamatory if republished if they had since separated and married other people.

DEALING WITH HYPERLINKS

There used to be a time when websites welcomed inbound links. And, although most hyperlinks are safe, there are increasing risks. Many websites will threaten legal action in order to prevent their content being accessed by an unauthorised link.

Most web users believe that website operators automatically give implied consent for people to link to any page they publish. But this is not always the case – especially when there's money to be made.

For instance, a link may bypass a paywall, or try to exploit a commercial advantage from another page.

Case study

One of the earliest cases on unauthorised linking was that of Shetland Times v Wills (Net Litigation, 1996, *Shetland Times, Ltd. v. Jonathan Wills and Another*).

From October 1996, the Shetland News website reproduced several news headlines from their rival publication, the Shetland Times. The Shetland News also hyperlinked these headlines to the Shetland Times webpages.

The Shetland Times argued that the Shetland News was breaching the Copyright, Designs and Patents Act by passing off Shetland Times stories as their own, and won an interim injunction at the Court of Session, Edinburgh, to stop practise.

Lord Hamilton said: "We all know that the homepage is the most popular area of a website. It is the gateway to the rest of the site.

"However, the ability to bypass the homepage and link directly to a certain web page is surely fundamental to the continued success of the internet. Indeed, entire businesses have been created by indexing individual pages" (BBC News, 1997, *Shetland Internet squabble settled out of court*).

The two parties eventually made a settlement, and the Shetland News agreed to acknowledge the ownership of any Shetland Times story which appeared on its website.

Twenty years later, the practise of acknowledging the ownership of hyperlinks is still a good way to avoid legal problems.

Generally, linking deep into a website, (such as linking to this webpage: www.examplewebsite.com/products/ /hoses/parts/) is more legally risky than simply linking to a homepage (www.examplewebsite.com), but web editors should be aware that any link to another website can present legal risks.

The legal dangers associated with hyperlinks are discussed below.

LIBEL

Journalists may face legal proceedings by providing links that draw people's attention to defamatory content on other websites.

Case study

The legal precedent for linking to other sites is based on a case that goes back more than 100 years to 1894. A man named Mr Wood sat by the side of a road pointing to a placard containing a defamatory statement about another man, Mr Hird.

It is unclear who wrote the statement. However, Hird sued Wood for libel, and the Court of Appeal decided that Wood was liable for publishing the statement, because he drew attention to it (Defamation Update, n.d., *The Solicitors Journal/Cases of the Week/Hird v Wood*).

This created the precedent that if publishers "point" readers to defamatory content, they may share legal responsibility as a publisher.

The Hird v Wood case was referred to in the 2010 libel case Spectator and Islam Expo (BAILII, EWHC 2011, 2010).

In a preliminary hearing, Mr Justice Tugendhat ruled that content accessed via links in an article in the Spectator should be treated as part of the offending article in the trial.

There are other subtleties involved in the Hirst v Wood case that help to inform web editors.

First, Wood actively encouraged people to read the sign, and obviously approved of the statement. In addition, he was situated in the same place as the placard.

Therefore, a hyperlink may be safe if it does not encourage people to read the page that it links to, nor suggest that the website agrees with the content.

And, it may also be possible to argue that another website is not in the same place as the original site.

Example

Linking to a defamatory article about "celebrity" Jason Dipstick on the Sun's website may be safe, because it lists the link without giving clues about the content of the Sun's article, and it does not actively encourage people to click.

For example, this may be safe: <u>See news from today's Sun</u>

Whereas *this* link would be riskier because it gives clues about the content and encourages people to click:

Who's a naughty boy then? <u>Read about Jason Dipstick's latest exploits</u>

Web editors should always check carefully before linking to defamatory content on other websites.

CONTEMPT OF COURT

Linking to an article on another website, even one based overseas, could prejudice someone's trial if proceedings were active, under the CCA 1981.

Because contempt by publication is a strict liability offence, it may be harder for web editors to argue that they were not responsible for any contempt.

Scottish journalists should beware of creating links from articles on a Scottish website to prejudicial stories on an English one, as contempt laws are applied more strictly in Scotland.

However, a link from a UK website to a story on a foreign website about a person standing trial abroad would be safe.

Hyperlinks to sites that breach an injunction or a reporting restriction may also be seen as contempt of court.

COPYRIGHT

A ruling by the ECJ in September 2016 means that it is not always safe under copyright law to publish hyperlinks to articles on other websites.

> ## *Case study*
>
> The decision in the case GS Media BV v Sanoma Media effectively creates a new form of copyright infringement.
>
> In October 2011, a Dutch website, GeenStijl, posted links to leaked photos from the Dutch version of Playboy. Playboy's publishers, Sanoma Media, repeatedly asked for the links to be removed and eventually sued GeenStijl and its parent company, GS Media, for a breach of copyright.
>
> The court agreed, as the website profited from the traffic that it generated. GeenStijl lost its argument that the ruling reduced their ability to report newsworthy information (Info Curia Case-law of the Court of Justice, 2016, *Case C-160/15 GS Media BV Sanoma Media Netherlands BV, Playboy Enterprises International Inc., Britt Geertruida Dekker*).

The ruling is binding on all EU member states, and raises the question: when does posting a hyperlink amount to a copyright infringement?

It is now the case that posting hyperlinks to copyright work published illegally on third-party sites as a commercial activity may be seen as a breach of copyright.

In future, website operators will have to check each hyperlink to make sure it does not lead to infringing content, and remove links quickly if they receive a take-down request.

The ruling will particularly affect media and news-oriented sites, which use links within articles and other content. Some publishers may feel it is not worth spending the time and money on checking each link and responding to additional take-down requests.

The judges said in their ruling: "[…] it is undisputed that GS Media provided the hyperlinks to the files containing the photos for profit and that Sanoma had not authorised the publication of those photos on the internet."

They accepted that hyperlinks were integral to the internet and its benefits for free information and expression, and that regular internet users may find it difficult to check whether they are posting links to authorised or unauthorised material.

However, they added: "In contrast, where it is established that such a person knew or ought to have known that the hyperlink he posted provides access to a work illegally published, for example owing to the fact that he was notified thereof by the copyright holders, the provision of that link constitutes a 'communication to the public'.

"Furthermore, when hyperlinks are posted for profit, it may be expected that the person who posted such a link should carry out the checks necessary to ensure that the work concerned is not illegally published."

See the court's statement on this PDF:

http://curia.europa.eu/jcms/upload/docs/application/pdf/2016-09/cp160092en.pdf

The ruling overturned a decision in a previous case, Svensson and others v Retriever Sverige AB in 2014, in which four Swedish journalists lost their case against a media monitoring and aggregation service which provided links to their articles that had been published on other websites (5RB, n.d., *Nils Svensson and Others v Retriever Sverige AB*).

TRADEMARKS

If a trademark is used in a link, the link text should include the ® symbol if the trademark is registered.

OTHER RISKS

Links to unlawful content that breaches privacy or confidentiality, incites racial or religious hatred, is obscene, or encourages or induces acts of terrorism, could also risk prosecution, although it must be stressed there are no legal precedents.

In all of these instances above, web editors will be more likely to face prosecution if:

1. The main purpose of a link is to refer readers to the unlawful material.

2. They know the content they are linking to is unlawful.

3. They actively refer people to it.

However, a link created automatically by a website tool is unlikely to create any legal danger.

MOBILE JOURNALISM AND THE TERRORISM ACT 2000

Several photographers and video journalists taking footage in public places have been confronted by police officers requesting that they stop taking photographs, and in some cases officers have attempted to confiscate equipment under section 44 of the Terrorism Act 2000 (UK Legislation, n.d., *Terrorism Act 2000*).

In July 2010, this section was officially suspended, but if journalists plan to take photographs or video footage in a public place, they should be aware of their rights which are listed on this website:

http://media.gn.apc.org/photo/guidelines.html

Another useful website is "I'm a Photographer, not a Terrorist!" which includes a "bust card" for journalists on this webpage: http://phnat.org/bust-card/ It explains what journalists should do if stopped by police in such circumstances.

Appendix

Abbreviations

ACTS	
CA	Communications Act
CCA	Contempt of Court Act
CDPA	Copyright Designs and Patents Act
CJA	Criminal Justice Act
CMA	Computer Misuse Act
DA	Defamation Act
DEA	Digital Economy Act
DMCA	US Digital Millennium Copyright Act
DPA	Data Protection Act
ECA	European Communities Act
EDA	Education Act
EIR	Environmental Information Regulations
FA	Fraud Act
FIOA	Freedom of Information Act
GDPR	General Data Protection Regulation
IPA	Investigatory Powers Act

PCA	Protection of Children Act
PHA	Protection from Harassment Act
RIPA	Regulation of Investigatory Powers Act
ROA	Rehabilitation of Offenders Act
SCA	Serious Crime Act
SOA	Sexual Offences Act
YJCEA	Youth Justice and Criminal Evidence Act

COURTS AND BODIES	
CJEU	Court of Justice of the European Union
EC	European Commission
ECHR	European Convention on Human Rights
ECJ	European Court of Justice (The court of the CJEU)
ECtHR	European Court of Human Rights
ECD	EU Electronic Commerce Directive
ICO	Information Commissioner's Office
IT	Information Tribunal
IPO	Intellectual Property Office
IPSO	Independent Press Standards Organisation (prev. PPC)
MoJ	Ministry of Justice

OTHER	
AG	Attorney General
CCL	Creative Commons License
Editors' code	Ipso Editors' Code of Practice
EEA	European Economic Area
IM	Instant messages
IP	Internet Protocol
T&Cs	Terms and Conditions
UGC	User Generated Content

BIBLIOGRAPHY

5RB (n.d.) *Flood v Times Newspapers Limited (SC) Reference [2012] UKSC 11* [Online]. Available at http://www.5rb.com/case/flood-v-times-newspapers-limited-sc/ (Accessed 25 August 2015).

5RB (n.d.) *Google Spain SL v Agencia Española de Protección de Datos* [Online]. Available at http://www.5rb.com/case/google-spain-sl-v-agencia-espanola-de-proteccion-de-datos/ (Accessed 21 August 2015).

5RB (n.d.) *Nils Svensson and Others v Retriever Sverige AB Reference C-466/12* [Online]. Available at http://www.5rb.com/case/nils-svensson-others-v-retriever-sverige-ab/ (Accessed 25 August 2015).

BAILII, C14510 (2011) *Court of Justice of the European Communities (including Court of First Instance Decisions) Painer v Standard Verlags GmbH (Area of Freedom, Security and Justice) [2011] EUECJ C-145/10 (12 April 2011)* [Online]. Available at http://www.bailii.org/eu/cases/EUECJ/2011/C14510_O.html (Accessed 24 March 2016).

BAILII, ECHR 135 (2016) *European Court of Human Rights Judgment: Magyar Tartalomszolgaltatok Egyesulete And Index.Hu Zrt V. Hungary ECHR 135 [2016](02 February 2016)* [Online.] Available at http://www.bailii.org/eu/cases/ECHR/2016/135.html (Accessed 18 March 2016).

BAILII, ECHR 586 (2015) *European Court of Human Rights Grand Chamber Judgment: Delfi As V. Estonia ECHR 586 [2015] (16 June 2015)* [Online.] Available at http://www.bailii.org/eu/cases/ECHR/2015/586.html (Accessed 18 March 2016).

BAILII, ECHR 941 (2013) *European Court of Human Rights Chamber Judgment: Delfi As V. Estonia ECHR 941 [2013] (10 October 2013)* [Online.] Available at http://www.bailii.org/eu/cases/ECHR/2013/941.html (Accessed 18 March 2016).

BAILII, EUECJ C-348/13 (2014) *Court of Justice of the European Communities (including Court of First Instance Decisions) BestWater International (Order)* **French Text** *[2014] EUECJ C-348/13_CO (21 October 2014)* [Online]. Available at http://www.bailii.org/eu/cases/EUECJ/2014/C34813_CO.html (Accessed 1 April 2016).

BAILII, EWCA Civ 100 (2016) *England and Wales Court of Appeal (Civil Division) Decisions PJS v News Group Newspapers Ltd [2016] EWCA Civ 100 (22 January 2016)* [Online]. Available at http://www.bailii.org/ew/cases/EWCA/Civ/2016/100.html (Accessed 13 April 2016).

BAILII, EWHC 145 (2013) *England and Wales High Court (Queen's Bench Division) Decisions: Cruddas v Adams EWHC 145 [2013] (QB) (04 February 2013)* [Online]. Available at http://www.bailii.org/ew/cases/EWHC/QB/2013/145.html (Accessed 21 August 2015).

BAILII, EWHC 1600(2) (2002) *England and Wales High Court (Queen's Bench Division) Decisions >> Lillie & Anor v Newcastle City Council & Ors [2002] EWHC 1600(2) (QB) (30 July 2002)* [Online]. Available at http://www.bailii.org/ew/cases/EWHC/QB/2002/1600(2).html (Accessed 4 January 2017).

BAILII, EWHC 183 (2016) *England and Wales High Court (Administrative Court) Decisions: Ewing v Crown Court Sitting at Cardiff & Newport & Ors [2016] EWHC 183 (Admin) (08 February 2016* [Online.] Available at http://www.bailii.org/ew/cases/EWHC/Admin/2016/183.html (Accessed 18 March 2016).

BAILII, EWHC 2011 (2010) *England and Wales High Court (Queen's Bench Division) Decisions Islam Expo Ltd v The Spectator (1828) Ltd & Anor [2010] EWHC 2011 (QB) (30 July 2010)* [Online]. Available at http://www.bailii.org/ew/cases/EWHC/QB/2010/2011.html (Accessed 13 April 2016).

BAILII, EWHC 2242 (2015) *England and Wales High Court (Queen's Bench Division) Decisions: Lachaux v Independent Print Ltd EWHC 2242 [2015] (QB) (30 July 2015)* [Online]Available at http://www.bailii.org/ew/cases/EWHC/QB/2015/2242.html (Accessed 16 March 2016).

BAILII, EWHC 2628 (2015) *England and Wales High Court (Queen's Bench Division) Decisions: Brett Wilson LLP v Person(s) Unknown, Responsible for the Operation and Publication of the Website www.solicitorsfromhelluk.com EWHC 2628 [2015] (QB) (16 September 2015)* [Online] Available at http://www.bailii.org/ew/cases/EWHC/QB/2015/2628.html (Accessed 17 March 2016).

BAILII, EWHC 2831 (2014) *England and Wales High Court (Queen's Bench Division) Decisions: Cooke & Anor v MGN Ltd & Anor EWHC 2831 [2014]* [Online] Available at http://www.bailii.org/ew/cases/EWHC/QB/2014/2831.html (Accessed 17 March 2016).

BAILII, EWHC 2981 (2012) *England and Wales High Court (Administrative Court) Decisions: Attorney General v Associated Newspapers Ltd & Anor EWHC 2981 [2012] (Admin) (16 October 2012)* [Online.] Available at http://www.bailii.org/ew/cases/EWHC/Admin/2012/2981.html (Accessed 18 March 2016).

BAILII, EWHC 3322 (2015) *England and Wales High Court (Administrative Court) Decisions: HM Attorney General v The Condé Nast Publications Ltd EWHC 3322 [2015] (Admin) (18 November 2015)* [Online.] Available at http://www.bailii.org/ew/cases/EWHC/Admin/2015/3322.html (Accessed 18 March 2016) .

BAILII, EWHC 3380 (2015) *England and Wales High Court (Queen's Bench Division) Decisions: Ahuja v Politika Novine I Magazini D.O.O & Ors EWHC 3380 [2015] (QB) (23 November 2015)* [Online.] Available at http://www.bailii.org/ew/cases/EWHC/QB/2015/3380.html (Accessed 4 April 2016).

BAILII, EWHC 3769 (2015) *England and Wales High Court (Queen's Bench Division) Decisions: Theedom v Nourish Training (t/a Recruitment Colin Sewell) EWHC 3769 [2015] (QB) (11 December 2015)* [Online] Available at http://www.bailii.org/ew/cases/EWHC/QB/2015/3769.html (Accessed 16 March 2016).

BAILII, EWHC 575 (2016) *England and Wales High Court (Chancery Division) Decisions England and Wales Cricket Board Ltd & Anor v Tixdaq Ltd & Anor [2016] EWHC 575 (Ch) (18 March 2016)* [Online]. Available at http://www.bailii.org/ew/cases/EWHC/Ch/2016/575.html (Accessed 30 March 2016).

BAILII, EWHC B24 (2014) *England and Wales High Court (Queen's Bench Division) Decisions: Johnson v Steele & Ors EWHC B24 [2014] (QB) (29 October 2014)* [Online]. Available at http://www.bailii.org/ew/cases/EWHC/QB/2014/B24.html (Accessed 21 August 2015).

BAILII, UKSC 11 (2012) *United Kingdom Supreme Court Judgment: Flood v Times Newspapers Ltd UKSC 11 [2012] (21 March 2012)* [Online.] Available at http://www.bailii.org/uk/cases/UKSC/2012/11.html (Accessed 17 March 2016).

BAILII, UKUT 139 (AAC) (2016) *Upper Tribunal (Administrative Appeals Chamber) DH v Information Commissioner & Anor (Information rights : Freedom of information - absolute exemptions) [2016] UKUT 139 (AAC) (10 March 2016)* [Online] Available at http://www.bailii.org/uk/cases/UKUT/AAC/2016/139/ (Accessed 5 April 2016).

BBC News (1997) *Shetland Internet squabble settled out of court* [Online]. Available at http://news.bbc.co.uk/1/hi/sci/tech/29191.stm (Accessed 20 April 2016).

BBC News (2010) *Edlington attack "could have been prevented"*) [Online]. Available at http://news.bbc.co.uk/1/mobile/programmes/newsnight/84599 38.stm (Accessed 5 January 2017).

BBC News (2014) *Runa Khan jailed for Facebook Syria terror posts* [Online]. Available at http://www.bbc.co.uk/news/uk-england-30439913 (Accessed 21 August 2015).

BBC News (2013) *Government requests to Facebook outlined in report* [Online]. Available at http://beta.bbc.co.uk/news/technology-23852230 (Accessed 6 January 2017).

BBC Radio 4 (2016) *The Media Show: Celebrity injunctions* [Online]. Available at http://www.bbc.co.uk/programmes/b064z78f (Accessed 5 January 2017).

Big Issue North (2015) *They don't scare me now* [Online]. Available at http://www.bigissuenorth.com/2015/08/they-dont-scare-me-now/14111 (Accessed 20 April 2016).

Blair, A. (2011) *A Journey*, London, The Random House Group, Cornerstone Publishing.

Carruthers Law (2013) *Lord McAlpine of West Green v Sally Bercow* [Online]. Available at http://www.carruthers-law.co.uk/news/lord-mcalpine-of-west-green-v-sally-bercow/#.Vdcl3flVhBd (Accessed 17 March 2016).

CMP (2016) *Sharma v Sharma EWHC 3349 (2014),* [Online]. Available at https://collegeofmediaandpublishing.sharepoint.com/_layouts/15/guestaccess.aspx?guestaccesstoken=hB4xyaj3YrEA2QU7zPLFth Eh%2bcwIDjvr2r60XWeNjX4%3d&docid=04f7fa180039e43f3b7 664790b46d63f2 (Accessed 17 March 2016).

Courts and Tribunals Judiciary (2012) *Weller -v- Associated Newspapers Ltd* [Online]. Available at https://www.judiciary.gov.uk/judgments/weller-v-associated-newspapers-ltd/ (Accessed 18 March 2016).

Courts and Tribunals Judiciary (2015) *Freddie Starr v Karin Ward* [Online]. Available at https://www.judiciary.gov.uk/judgments/57319/ (Accessed 24 August 2015).

Courts and Tribunals Judiciary, 2016, *Economou v de Freitas [2016] EWHC 1853 (QB)*) [Online]. Available at https://www.judiciary.gov.uk/judgments/economou-v-de-freitas-2016-ewhc-1853-qb/ (Accessed 6 January 2017).

Courts NI (2015) *CG v Facebook Ireland Ltd. [2015] NIQB 11* [Online]. Available at https://www.courtsni.gov.uk/en-GB/Judicial%20Decisions/PublishedByYear/Documents/2015/%5B2015%5D%20NIQB%2011/j_j_STE9491Final.htm (Accessed 5 January 2017).

Courts NI, 2015, *Court awards damages against Joseph Mccloskey and Facebook for identifying sex offender: Summary of Judgment* [Online]. Available at https://www.courtsni.gov.uk/en-GB/Judicial%20Decisions/SummaryJudgments/Documents/Court%20awards%20damages%20against%20Joseph%20McCloskey%20and%20Facebook%20for%20identifying%20sex%20offender/j_j_Summary%20of%20judgment%20-%20%20CG%20v%20Facebook%20and%20Joseph%20McCloskey%2020%20Feb%2015.htm (Accessed 6 January 2017).

CPS (2009) *Contempt of Court and Reporting Restrictions: Strict Liability Contempt under the Contempt of Court Act 1981* [Online]. Available at http://www.cps.gov.uk/legal/a_to_c/contempt_of_court/#a12 (Accessed 21 August 2015).

Defamation Update (n.d.) *The Solicitors Journal/Cases of the Week/Hird v Wood* [Online]. PDF available at http://defamationupdate.co.nz/sites/all/pdf/CaseoftheMonth/Hird-v-Wood-1894-38-SJ-234.pdf (Accessed 13 April 2016).

European Commission (2009) *C-5/08 Infopaq International A/S v Danske Dagblades Forening, judgment of 16 July 2009* [Online]. PDF available at http://ec.europa.eu/dgs/legal_service/arrets/08c005_en.pdf (Accessed 25 August 2015).

European Commission (2015) *A Digital Single Market Strategy for Europe* [Online]. Available at http://eur-lex.europa.eu/legal-content/EN/TXT/?uri=celex%3A52015DC0192 (Accessed 22 March 2016).

European Commission (2016) *Digital Single Market* [Online]. Available at https://ec.europa.eu/digital-single-market/en/news/summary-report-public-consultation-evaluation-and-review-regulatory-framework-electronic (Accessed 22 March 2016).

European Commission (2016) *Guidelines on Data Protection Officers* [Online]. PDF available at http://ec.europa.eu/information_society/newsroom/image/document/2016-51/wp243_en_40855.pdf (Accessed 10 January 2017).

European Court of Human Rights (2013) *Case of Putistin v. Ukraine* [Online]. Available at http://hudoc.echr.coe.int/eng?i=001-128204#{"itemid":["001-128204"]} (Accessed 24 August 2015).

Facebook (2015) *Global Government Requests Report* [Online]. Available at https://www.facebook.com/about/government_requests (Accessed 21 August 2015).

Facebook (2016) *Campaigner tells court she did not provoke alleged kick* [Online]. Available at https://www.facebook.com/sthelensstar/posts/1180474945332525 (Accessed 5 January 2017).

Freedom House (2016) *Silencing the Messenger: Communication Apps Under Pressure*) [Online]. Available at https://freedomhouse.org/report/freedom-net/freedom-net-2016 (Accessed 03 January 2017).

GOV.UK (2013) *Defamation Act 2013* [Online]. Available at http://www.legislation.gov.uk/ukpga/2013/26 (Accessed 5 January 2017).

GOV.UK (2014) *Changes to Copyright Law* [Online] PDF available at https://www.gov.uk/government/publications/changes-to-copyright-law (Accessed 5 January 2017).

GOV.UK (2015) *Draft Investigatory Powers Bill* [Online]. Available at https://www.gov.uk/government/publications/draft-investigatory-powers-bill (Accessed 18 March 2016).

GOV.UK (n.d.) *Intellectual Property Office IPO* [Online]. Available at https://www.gov.uk/government/organisations/intellectual-property-office (Accessed 25 August 2015).

Hold the Front Page (2016) *Wrightson judge explains why he kept killers' names secret* [Online]. Available at http://www.holdthefrontpage.co.uk/2016/news/wrightson-judge-explains-why-he-kept-killers-names-secret/ (Accessed 13 April 2016).

ICO (2015) *CO orders removal of Google search results* [Online]. Available at https://ico.org.uk/about-the-ico/news-and-events/news-and-blogs/2015/08/ico-orders-removal-of-google-search-results/ (Accessed 18 March 2016).

ICO (2015) *Google Inc* [Online]. Available at https://ico.org.uk/action-weve-taken/enforcement/google-inc/ (accessed 4 April 2016).

ICO (2016) *Data protection and journalism: a guide for the media* [Online]. Available at https://ico.org.uk/media/for-organisations/documents/1552/data-protection-and-journalism-media-guidance.pdf (Accessed 4 January 2017).

ICO (n.d.) *When can we refuse a request for information?* [Online]. Available at https://ico.org.uk/for-organisations/guide-to-freedom-of-information/refusing-a-request/ (Accessed 25 August 2015).

ICO News Blog (2016) *Information Commissioner updates on WhatsApp / Facebook investigation* [Online]. Available at https://iconewsblog.wordpress.com/2016/11/07/information-commissioner-updates-on-whatsapp-facebook-investigation/ (Accessed 5 January 2017).

Info Curia Case-law of the Court of Justice (2015) *Pez Hejduk v. EnergieAgentur. NRW GmbH, Case C-441/13* [Online]. Available at http://curia.europa.eu/juris/document/document.jsf?docid=1616 11&doclang=EN (Accessed 25 August 2015).

Info Curia Case-law of the Court of Justice (2016) *Case C-160/15 GS Media BV Sanoma Media Netherlands BV, Playboy Enterprises International Inc., Britt Geertruida Dekker* [Online]. Available at http://curia.europa.eu/juris/document/document.jsf?text=&doci d=175626&pageIndex=0&doclang=EN&mode=req&dir=&occ= first&part=1&cid=909494 (Accessed 20 April 2016).

Information Tribunal (2015) *Appeal No: EA/2014/0265*) [Online]. PDF available at http://www.informationtribunal.gov.uk/DBFiles/Decision/i1527 /Wall,%20Tom%20EA.2014.0265%20%2813.04.15%29.pdf (Accessed 20 April 2016).

Information Tribunal (2016) *Steve Pritchard and Information Commissioner EA/2015/0175* [Online]. PDF available at http://www.informationtribunal.gov.uk/DBFiles/Decision/i1750 /Pritchard,Steve%20EA-2015-0175%20(11-03-16- %20OPEN)%20.pdf (Accessed 5 April 2016).

IPlens (2016) *Right to be forgotten: the first Italian decision after Google Spain* [Online]. Available at https://iplens.org/2016/01/18/right-to-be-forgotten-the-first-italian-decision-after-google-spain/ (Accessed 13 April 2016).

Ipso (2015) *Editors' Code of Practice* [Online]. Available at https://www.ipso.co.uk/IPSO/cop.html (Accessed 24 August 2015).

Ipso (2016) *03446-16 McHale v The Sun* [Online]. Available at https://www.ipso.co.uk/rulings-and-resolution-statements/ruling/?id=03446-16 (Accessed 4 January 2017).

National Constitution Center (n.d.) *Amendment I Freedom of religion, speech, press, assembly, and petition* [Online]. Available at http://constitutioncenter.org/constitution/the-amendments/amendment-1-freedom-of-religion-press-expression (Accessed 21 August 2015).

NCA (2016) *Help available for webcam blackmail victims: don't panic, and don't pay* [Online]. Available at http://www.nationalcrimeagency.gov.uk/index.php/news-media/nca-news/960-help-available-for-webcam-blackmail-victims-don-t-panic-and-don-t-pay (Accessed 5 January 2017).

Net Litigation (1996) *Shetland Times, Ltd. v. Jonathan Wills and Another* [Online]. Available at http://www.netlitigation.com/netlitigation/cases/shetland.htm (Accessed 20 April 2016).

Pink News (2006) *Ashley Cole files lawsuit over gay orgy story* [Online]. (Available at http://www.pinknews.co.uk/2006/03/03/ashley-cole-files-lawsuit-over-gay-orgy-story/ (Accessed 21 August 2015).

Pinsent Masons Out-Law.com (2013) *Privacy rights existed despite RocknRoll Facebook photos being accessible by public, rules High Court* [Online]. Available at http://www.out-law.com/en/articles/2013/january/privacy-rights-existed-despite-rocknroll-facebook-photos-being-accessible-by-public-rules-high-court/ (Accessed 21 August 2015).

Press Gazette (2015) *Research finds 27 per cent drop in reported libel cases since Defamation Act 2013* [Online]. Available at http://www.pressgazette.co.uk/content/research-finds-27-cent-drop-reported-libel-cases-defamation-act-2014 (Accessed 24 March 2016).

Press Gazette (2015) *RIPA report shocks industry, but leaves journalists targeted by police in the dark* [Online]. Available at http://www.pressgazette.co.uk/ripa-report-shocks-industry-leaves-journalists-targeted-police-dark (Accessed 21 August 2015).

Press Gazette (2016) *Likening Alan Sugar to "spiv" Sir Philip Green in headline costs Daily Mail £20,000* [Online]. Available at http://www.pressgazette.co.uk/likening-alan-sugar-to-spiv-sir-philip-green-in-headline-costs-daily-mail-20000/ (Accessed 4 January 2017).

Press Gazette (2016) *NUJ: Investigatory Powers Bill is "profound threat to public's right to know"* [Online]. Available at http://www.pressgazette.co.uk/nuj-lack-source-safeguards-investigatory-powers-bill-profound-threat-publics-right-know (Accessed 22 March 2016).

Press Gazette (2016) *When government press officers think they are court reporters justice could be the loser* [Online]. Available at http://www.pressgazette.co.uk/journalists-beware-of-government-press-officers-who-think-they-are-court-reporters/ (Accessed 5 January 2017).

Reporters Without Borders (2016) *2016 World Press Freedom Index* [Online]. Available at http://rsf.org/ranking (Accessed 20 April 2016).

Schillings (2014) *Landmark Facebook libel case* [Online]. Available at https://www.schillings.co.uk/news-and-opinion/landmark-facebook-libel-case (Accessed 17 March 2016).

Society of Editors (2016) *New alert over internet comment contempt risk* [Online]. Available at https://www.societyofeditors.org/soe-news/13-april-2016/new-alert-over-internet-comment-contempt-risk (Accessed 19 April 2016).

The Guardian (1999) *Aitken jailed for 18 months* [Online]. Available at http://www.theguardian.com/politics/1999/jun/08/uk (Accessed 8 April 2016).

The Guardian (2006) *England footballer sues tabloids* [Online].
Available at
http://www.theguardian.com/media/2006/mar/02/pressandpubl
ishing.football (Accessed 21 August 2015).

The Guardian (2013) *Google, Facebook and Twitter ordered to delete
photos of James Bulger killers* [Online]. Available at
http://www.theguardian.com/media/2013/feb/26/google-
facebook-twitter (Accessed 21 August 2015).

The Guardian (2014) *Paul Weller children win privacy damages over
photos on Mail Online* [Online]. Available at
https://www.theguardian.com/music/2014/apr/16/paul-weller-
privacy-damages-children-photos-mail-online (Accessed 4 January
2017).

The Guardian (2014) *Plebgate: Met obtained phone records of Sun political
editor without consent* [Online]. Available at
http://www.theguardian.com/media/2014/sep/02/plebgate-met-
phone-records-sun-tom-newton-dunn (Accessed 24 August 2015).

The Guardian (2014) *Police secretly obtained reporter's phone records in
Huhne investigation* [Online]. Available at
http://www.theguardian.com/uk-news/2014/oct/05/police-
chris-huhne-reporter-phone-records (Accessed 24 August 2015).

The Guardian (2014) *Ukip MEP apologises for apparently calling charity
boss a paedophile* [Online]. Available at
http://www.theguardian.com/politics/2014/nov/01/ukip-mep-
apologises-tweet-charity-boss-paedophile (Accessed 21 August
2015).

The Guardian (2015) *Google accidentally reveals data on "right to be
forgotten" requests* [Online]. Available at
http://www.theguardian.com/technology/2015/jul/14/google-
accidentally-reveals-right-to-be-forgotten-requests (Accessed 21
August 2015).

The Guardian (2015) *GQ article* [Online.] Available at
http://www.theguardian.com/law/2015/jul/06/gq-article-phone-
hacking-trial-contempt-court (Accessed 18 March 2016).

The Guardian (2016) *Investigatory powers bill not up to the task* [Online]. Available at http://www.theguardian.com/law/2016/mar/14/investigatory-powers-bill-not-up-to-the-task (Accessed 22 March 2016).

The Guardian (2016) *Newsquest hit by growing copyright claims over use of photographs* [Online]. Available at https://www.theguardian.com/media/greenslade/2016/jul/27/newsquest-hit-by-growing-copyright-claims-over-use-of-photographs (Accessed 5 January 2016).

The Sun (2016) *Dad's anger after commuters refused to help son* [Online]. Available at https://www.thesun.co.uk/news/1235550/dads-anger-after-commuters-refused-to-help-son-and-even-ran-over-his-body-on-motorway-after-bridge-fall/ (Accessed 4 January 2017).

The Telegraph (2013) *Steps star H wins public apology after being wrongly pictured as paedophile* [Online]. Available at http://www.telegraph.co.uk/news/uknews/law-and-order/10527588/Steps-star-H-wins-public-apology-after-being-wrongly-pictured-as-paedophile.html (Accessed 1 April 2016).

The Telegraph (2017) *Cheryl Fernandez-Versini's husband wins magazine privacy damages* [Online]. Available at http://www.telegraph.co.uk/news/celebritynews/11304031/Cheryl-Coles-husband-wins-magazine-privacy-damages.html (Accessed 4 January 2017).

They Work for You (2016) *Social Networking: Photographs* [Online]. Available at http://www.theyworkforyou.com/wrans/?id=2015-10-19.12484.h&s=speaker%3A11905#g12484.r0 (Accessed 30 March 2016).

Twitter (2015) *Transparency Report: Removal Requests* [Online]. Available at https://transparency.twitter.com/removal-requests/2015/jan-jun (Accessed 21 August 2015).

UK Legislation (n.d.) *Copyright, Designs and Patents Act 1988* [Online]. Available at http://www.legislation.gov.uk/ukpga/1988/48/contents (Accessed 25 August 2015).

UK Legislation (n.d.) *Criminal Justice and Courts Act 2015* [Online]. Available at http://www.legislation.gov.uk/ukpga/2015/2/section/72/enacted (Accessed 21 August 2015).

UK Legislation (n.d.) *Defamation Act 2013* [online]. Available at http://www.legislation.gov.uk/ukpga/2013/26/contents (Accessed 24 August 2015).

UK Legislation (n.d.) *Human Rights Act 1998 Article 10* [Online]. Available at http://www.legislation.gov.uk/ukpga/1998/42/schedule/1/part/I/chapter/9 (Accessed 21 August 2015).

UK Legislation (n.d.) *Terrorism Act 2000* [Online]. Available at http://www.legislation.gov.uk/ukpga/2000/11/section/44 (Accessed 25 August 2015).

UK Parliament (n.d.) *Digital Economy Bill (HL Bill 80)* [Online]. Available at http://www.publications.parliament.uk/pa/bills/lbill/2016-2017/0080/lbill_2016-20170080_en_1.htm (Accessed 5 January 2017).

UK Parliament House of Lords (n.d.) *Judgments – Reynolds v. Times Newspapers Limited and Others* [Online]. Available at http://www.publications.parliament.uk/pa/ld199899/ldjudgmt/jd991028/rey01.htm (Accessed 21 August 2015).

What do they know (n.d.) *Browse And Search Requests* [Online]. Available at https://www.whatdotheyknow.com/list/all?#results (Accessed 25 August 2015).

COURSES IN MEDIA LAW

Cleland Thom is principal of the College of Media and Publishing, which is one of the UK's largest providers of accredited online courses in proofreading, journalism, writing and marketing.

CMP delivers courses leading to the NCTJ diploma: http://collegeofmediaandpublishing.co.uk/nctj-diploma, as well as a range of courses in law, where students can work with Cleland as tutor, including:

1. Internet law.

2. Media law basics.

3. Media law refresher.

For details see: http://collegeofmediaandpublishing.co.uk/

Printed in Poland
by Amazon Fulfillment
Poland Sp. z o.o., Wrocław